How to Manage Your Money, or Down and Out in Athens, Ohio

David Bruce

While every precaution has been taken in the preparation of this book, the publisher assumes no responsibility for errors or omissions, or for damages resulting from the use of the information contained herein.

HOW TO MANAGE YOUR MONEY, OR DOWN AND OUT IN ATHENS, OHIO

First edition. October 21, 2022.

Table of Contents

How to Manage Your Money: A Guide for the Non-Rich

Preface

Your net worth is simply what you are worth in terms of money. Too many of us have a negative net worth or very little positive net worth. If you've just graduated from college or from high school, you probably haven't gotten very far in building the wealth that you would like to have in the future (or now!).

This book was written to help you get a net worth with which you can be happy. It was written for the person just starting out, who is just beginning to make money and who wants to use that money wisely. It assumes that you aren't a millionaire — many finance books have already been written for rich people.

Following the advice in this document won't make anyone rich, but it should help many people. Some risk is involved, but the advice should be sound. You, of course, will have to decide whether to use this advice. You certainly don't have to invest in a mutual fund at Fidelity, T. Rowe Price, Vanguard, or anywhere else. And, of course, I am not responsible for any losses that a mutual fund or other investment may suffer. You make your own investment decisions, and you have the responsibility for them.

Chapter 1: How to Learn the Basics

1. Know Your Net Worth

Net worth is one of the few economic terms used in this book (two others are assets and liabilities, and two more are income and expenses). Your statement of net worth consists of two sections.

First is your list of assets, which are the things you own which are worth money. Under assets, you list such things as the money in your checking and savings accounts, the worth of your car and other household belongings, etc. (If your statement of net worth were a Western movie, your assets would be the good guys in the white hats.)

Second is your list of liabilities, which are the debts you owe (the bad guys in the black hats). If you took out a loan to buy a car, the amount you still owe is a liability and would be listed on the liability side of your net worth statement. If you just got out of college, you probably were forced to get loans to help pay for your college degree. Those loans are also liabilities.

To figure up your net worth, add up your liabilities and subtract that amount from the amount of your total assets. Voila! You now know what you are worth in terms of money. If your net worth is positive, wonderful. You are worth more than you owe. On the other hand, if you just graduated or think that credit cards are the best thing since David Letterman started dropping watermelons from tall buildings, at least you know from where you're starting.

In either case, you now have a snapshot of where you stand financially. You should take that snapshot periodically — at least every year. You need to figure out your net worth to determine whether the rats are winning, you and the rats are staying about even, or you're a big cheese.

It's too much to say that your net worth is a measurement of your score in life (in business, maybe), but having at least a little money is better than having none at all.

2. Know Your Income and Expenses

Here are two more economic terms to learn: income and expenses. Income is all the money you have coming in; expenses are all the money, except that flowing into savings and investments, you have going out. You figure out your income and expenses to find out about a third item: net income, or the difference between your income and your expenses. If your expenses are more than your income, you have a negative net income — and perhaps a very serious problem. (Going into debt in order to get a good education that will lead to a good job is acceptable; going into debt so that you can buy more toys that you really don't care that much for is unacceptable.) If your income is less than your expenses, you have a positive net income — and probably a positive outlook on life.

You need to keep an income/expense statement: a statement of your income and your expenses. This statement serves two purposes: one concerning the past, and one concerning the future. First, it serves as a map of where your money has gone. Second, it serves to help you make a plan of where you want your money to go. Both purposes will help you to budget.

Keeping this statement need not be too difficult. At the end of each day write down where you spent your money. Use broad categories such as groceries, rent, eating outside the home, entertainment, reading material. Also, don't worry about keeping track of every last penny. If you can't remember whether you paid $13.50 or $14.50 for that book, call it $14.

It's a good idea to have your own computer with your own copy of a personal finance computer program such as *Quicken*, which will help you keep track of your income and your expenses and will give you a statement of your net worth.

3. Budget

You need to budget for one simple reason: to increase your net income. Your savings and investments come out of your net income, and savings and investments are what make rich people rich and well-off people well off. (Expenses, on the other hand, are often what make poor people poor.)

By keeping a record of where your money goes, you will find those places where you can cut back. You will probably find that you are spending money on things that add nothing to your life, that are junk — or are things that are OK, but you can find better things on which to spend your money. Once you identify the things that are junk, you know to avoid spending money on them. Once you avoid spending money on the things that are worthless, you will have available more money to spend and invest. Once you have money to save and invest, you will have more money to spend on the things that are worthwhile.

It's funny, but by resisting the urge to spend money on junk now, you will have more money to spend on worthwhile things in the future.

To make a realistic budget, keep track of your expenses, at least for a month. After you do this, your expenses for such luxuries as eating in restaurants will probably shock you. (On the other hand, if you consider eating in restaurants a necessity, you may be shocked by the amount of money you spend on such luxuries as groceries.)

Then make up a list of your income for the following month. (This should be easy enough, if you're on salary as are most people.) Next make up a list of all your necessary, fixed (meaning you have to pay them at regular times, whether you want to or not) expenses, such as rent, house and/or car payments, etc. This should also be easy since they are fixed.

Finally comes the hardest part of the three: Make up a list of non-fixed expenses — that is, expenses you have some control over. Doing this will be easier because you have made an income/expense statement for last month. When you do your planning in this area, you will be aware of what happened to your money last month. If you don't like some of the places where your money went last month, you can

make sure that this month you spend less in those areas by monitoring
how much you're spending and where you're spending it.

A budget and an income/expense statement should be made up
each month. Last month's income/expense statement will help you
make up next month's budget.

One very important point: Make sure that you make a place for
savings when you make up your budget. You definitely don't want to
spend every penny you make. In fact, savings should be the first item of
your budget.

Of course, a computer program such as *Quicken* can easily create
a budget for you if you enter your income and expenses into the
program. It's a good idea to sit down in the evening each day and enter
the amount of money you have spent and what you spent it on.

4. Pay Yourself First

How do you avoid not spending every penny you make, especially
today in the age of modern advertising?

There is one simple rule you can follow: Pay yourself first. Lots of
people have claims on the money you make: the taxman, the landlord,
the bank, the finance company, etc. — sometimes it seems as if that
"etc." includes everybody but you.

That's not right; after all, you make the money. One way to get out
of this dilemma is to pay yourself first. That doesn't mean to splurge on
yourself at the beginning of the month because, after all, it always seems
as if there's never any money at the end of the month. Instead, it means
to put some money away in a savings account or some other place at
the beginning of the month because otherwise there never will be any
money at the end of the month. You've got to have a savings plan.

5. Have a Savings Plan

You have to plan ahead to save; otherwise, it won't get done. If
possible, you should plan on saving 10 percent of your take-home
income. It can be done — the Japanese save much more than 10
percent.

By saving the money at the first of the month — or whenever you get paid — you will soon form the habit of saving. Once the habit is formed, it's easy to keep up. Getting started is the hard part.

You may not realize this, but living on 90 percent of your income is almost the same as living on 100 percent of your income in the short run. And in the long run, of course, when the money you will have saved has a chance to earn interest and the interest it has earned has a chance to earn interest, then your standard of living will be much higher than if you had spent every penny you made.

One good formula for budgeting is the 10-20-70 rule. According to this rule, 10 percent of your take-home income is (or should be) for long-term (do not touch until you retire) savings, 20 percent is savings for big-ticket (expensive) items such as a car (or the 20 percent may be used to get yourself out of debt, if you are just beginning to get serious about your money), and 70 percent is for living expenses. Savings for a down payment on a house would come from the 20 percent of your salary earmarked for big-ticket items. Once you buy the house, the mortgage payment could come from both the long-term savings part (for the equity in your home) and from the living-expenses part of your budget (for the interest on the mortgage).

6. Have an Emergency Fund

The first thing you will do when you begin saving is to start an emergency fund. This will be the core of your savings, which you will put in a safe place such as a Federal Deposit Insurance Corporation (FDIC)-insured bank (in other words, the federal government guarantees that if the bank collapses financially while your money — any amount up to $100,000 for an individual — is in it, you will get your money back). Your emergency savings should be the equivalent of at least two months of your take-home salary. As you grow older, you will continue to add to the emergency fund (after all, two months' take-home salary will grow larger as your earning power increases), and you may even make it six or more months of your take-home salary.

Your emergency fund is for just that: emergencies. If you get hurt in a car accident, or are suddenly transferred, or your boss asks you to do something ethically unsavory and you quit, or you get hit by lightning not of the intellectual kind, or whatever, you've got some money to pay the bills until the insurance or Social Security checks start coming in.

7. Make a Will

Even if you're single and even if you have a negative net worth, you should make a will. Although you may be loaded to the gills with debt, you probably still have things that members of your family would like to have if you should die suddenly — would Aunt Edna want those embarrassing bare-butt baby photos of yourself that you keep hidden in the overnight case in the closet? If so, you might as well leave them to her.

When you make a will, you simply go to a lawyer to have a document made up that states whom you want to get what should you die. This need not be time-consuming or expensive. My simple (everything to be divided equally among my surviving brothers and sisters) will, which I had made up when I had a net worth of only a couple of thousand dollars, cost only $25. (Of course, it was a long time ago.) Even though my net worth is now much higher, I still haven't found it necessary to have my will changed, although it will be easy to make alterations should the time come.

Another advantage of having a will is that you can put final wishes in it. For example, I asked that donations be made to charity in lieu of flowers. (By the way, I don't want a funeral; I have donated my body to the Ohio University School of Osteopathic Medicine.) However, it's important that your wishes be communicated to the executor (the person you charge with carrying out your wishes as listed in the will) of your will before you die; otherwise, the decision to give you an expensive funeral with loads of flowers may be made before your will is read.

8. Make a Living Will

Make a living will. A living will is a document that will make known what kind of medical decisions you want made for you when it comes to life-prolonging medical treatments.

What happens if, God forbid, you go into a coma from which you are not expected to awake? You will be incapacitated and unable to make your own judgments. In your living will, you can state what decisions you want to be made for you. You can state that you don't want expensive, life-prolonging treatment, or that you do want expensive, life-prolonging treatment, or that you do want expensive, life-prolonging treatment for only a certain period of time.

One reason to make a living will is to spare your relatives the pain of wondering whether they made the right decision on your behalf. In your living will, you can spell out the decision to make.

You can also make a document that gives your health care power of attorney to a trusted relative or other person. You may be incapacitated and unable to express your wishes but your health is not so dire that you have a terminal illness or are in a permanent vegetative state (in those, the living will comes into effect). If you have given your health care power of attorney to a trusted relative or other person, that person will be able to make decisions on your behalf.

9. Work Together

It's important that you share your financial details and end-of-life desires with someone. If you suddenly die, someone ought to know where you've saved or invested your money, where your insurance documents are, etc. Suffering a death in the family is terrible enough without also having to worry about uncovering a complicated trail of financial papers.

If you are married, certainly your spouse ought to know and understand your finances. Leaving a lot of insurance isn't enough; your spouse ought also to know how to handle money. What better way to learn than by working on finances together. So, if you are married, both of you ought to be familiar with the household finances and investments. If you're not married, a significant other or relative ought to know about your finances.

Even if you are single and without a significant other, you still need to leave a record of your finances and investments. My will is on file at my lawyer's (the filing fee is part of the $25 I paid her when she made up the will). I also sent copies of my will to my two brothers, whom I named co-executors of my will. My essential papers, including my will, are kept in my safety deposit box at my bank. In my safety deposit box, I have written a letter to my two brothers. In this letter, which I update every year or so, I spell out where my money is invested, complete with addresses and telephone numbers of my mutual funds, etc. When I die, they will know where all my investments and savings are located.

Chapter 2: How to Get Out (and Stay Out) of Debt

1. Control Your Expenses

If you are seriously in debt, or are just uncomfortable with the debt you have, you need to get rid of some of that debt. Bankruptcy is one way to get out of debt, but it can be, and often is, a dishonorable way. The honorable way to get out of debt is to pay off your debts. It's only fair that if you buy something, you pay for it.

Paying off debts means paying out money. So the problem is, how to get more money? There are two ways: 1) reduce (which means taking control of) your expenses, and 2) increase your income. Reducing your expenses is usually the easiest.

Preparing a budget and keeping a record of your income and expenses are two of your major weapons against unnecessary expenses. Keeping a record of income and expenses makes you aware where the unnecessary expenditures are, and making a budget means making a plan to avoid spending for those unnecessary expenses.

Another major weapon against unnecessary expenses is the ability to say no. Once you know that you spend too much money on eating out, for example, you need to decide not to eat out as often and then stick to your decision. You can come up with personal strategies about how to do this. Buying prepared foods is expensive compared with buying the ingredients needed to cook from scratch, yet the prepared foods are much cheaper than restaurant food. You can start cutting expenses by eating prepared foods at home, then, if you need to reduce expenses further, you can decide to do more cooking from scratch.

Saying no to minor purchases is an easy way to cut down on expenses. Joining a record or book club means spending money that you may want to spend elsewhere. If the brochure didn't come every month, perhaps you wouldn't have bought those albums you never play anymore or bought those books you still haven't read. (I love the library, not book clubs.)

It's the small purchases that dribble your money away that hurt most of us. Because we spend money on the little things, we never have money to get the big things. Many of us are being nickel-and-dimed to death.

However, if you can save money on the big things, do so. Can you shop around for cheaper car insurance? Can you get by with basic cable TV instead of having all the extras? Can entertainment be a DVD and a couple of steaks at home instead of an expensive evening out? Can you reduce bills by having fewer telephones or TVs?

2. Increase Your Income

Increasing your income is usually much more difficult than controlling your expenses and much more time consuming. It also can be much harder physically because most of us sell our labor. Still, there are ways to pick up some extra money here and there.

When I was in college, I was a very good student academically but a very poor student financially. So I made up an advertising flyer on my typewriter (this was before the days of the Macintosh), copied it (I may want to work for Xerox someday, so I didn't write that I 'Xeroxed' it), then gave it out to my professors. This led to several small jobs such as painting, raking leaves, and cleaning out basements and garages. It also led to one of my nicest small enterprises.

You see, many professors tend to do a lot of travelling, but these same professors have homes, pets, and plants. So they hired me to look after them. I was getting $6 a day to stay in a professor's home, eat his perishable food, watch his TV, and oh yes, feed and play with the pets and water the plants. This was great for me, and great for the professor, because it kept the pets, plants, and the home insurance man happy. Since I never held any wild parties in their homes, I got a good reputation and soon was making a few hundred dollars a year housesitting for a small circle of professors.

This employment brought me some much-needed money and also brought me closer to these professors (and their pets).

Be careful, though, if you start spending the money you make from working odd jobs or a second job, or from selling items from a profitable hobby, you may start relying on that money. Use the money to reduce your debt or to increase your savings. Don't use it to increase your expenses.

3. Avoid Unnecessary Installment Debt

Not all debt is created equal. Some debt is necessary and desirable. Few people can buy a car without using credit, and hardly anyone can buy a house without using credit. But using credit to buy a stereo system? Come on! If you really want a stereo system, save up for it, then buy it with cash. If you don't want a stereo system enough to be willing to save for a stereo system, then you don't really want a stereo system.

When you need to decide whether to use credit, consider whether what you want will contribute measurably to your earning power. Education — especially practical education in such things as nursing — usually will, so you can probably justify going into debt to pay tuition now so you can get greater earning power later. A house contributes immensely to your quality of life, so going into manageable debt to buy a house is worthwhile. But going into debt to buy a TV or a VCR or a vacation or most other things is plain foolish.

4. Burn (or Control) Your Credit Cards

With interest on credit card debt running at 19 percent (or more), who needs credit cards? One of the smartest things you can do is to burn your credit cards. Nobody needs credit that's very easy (and tempting) to get, and nobody needs to pay 19 percent on that credit.

If you pay just the minimum on your credit card bill this month (your company will smilingly say there's no hurry to pay it all off), the rest of the statement will come around again next month, with interest charges added — and probably with the charge for all the new things you've bought since last month. It keeps getting bigger and bigger.

You say that you think having a credit card is necessary in the 21th century? I don't believe that is strictly true for most people, but if you do (you may shop online), then the least you can do is have just one credit card, seldom use it, and always pay your debt promptly. But if you are uncomfortable with the debt you have now, burn your credit cards.

5. Pay Your Bills On Time

My mother never paid all her utility bills on time. The next month, the unpaid bill (or bills) would come again, with a late charge — and with another month's charge for water, gas, electricity, whatever. So my mother would pay the bills she had to pay to keep the utilities going, meaning that because of the late charges she had to let some other bills go that month. These bills would re-arrive the next month, with a late charge and a charge for another month's worth of gas or electricity or whatever ... etc. My mother ended up paying a fortune in late fees; if she had paid her utility bills promptly, when they were due, she would have avoided a great deal of aggravation, and she would have had more money to buy the things she and her kids wanted.

Don't get me wrong. I love my mother. I learned a lot from her. However, one of the things I learned, through her horrible example, was to take care of my money.

Pay your bills — especially those bills to which late charges are added or on which interest is charged — on time.

Unfortunately, some companies seem to want you to pay bills late so that they can collect late fees. My telephone company sent the bills to me in envelopes that look like they contain advertising, not a bill. Occasionally, I wouldn't open the envelope, with the result that I got hit by a late fee. Now that company is my ex-telephone company.

6. Keep Making Payments on Your Debt

Your debt may seem to you bigger than Godzilla, but continual payments can whittle it to down to size. Pay something, no matter how little, on your debts, no matter how big. When I took over my mother's finances, she had a large hospital bill. We paid $5 a month (all we could afford, because of all the other debts which we were making payments on) for a long time. As the number and size of her debts decreased, we were able to increase our payments to the hospital. Eventually, it — and all her other debts — were paid off.

One exception to this can be credit-card debt. It is possible to make payments each month, yet have the outstanding debt go up each month because of interest. In such a case, you will probably want to pay off your debt with the highest interest rates first.

7. Don't Get in Debt in the First Place

Of course, the best thing to do is not to get in debt in the first place, unless you have a good reason for getting into debt (such as getting an education or buying a house or car). Unfortunately, too many college students will fill out an application in order to get a free T-shirt, but then they end up getting in unnecessary debt because they have a credit card. That free T-shirt ends up being very expensive. If you can resist getting the free T-shirt, and if you can resist getting a credit card, you can resist getting into the credit-card debt in the first place.

Chapter 3: How to Handle Your Cash

1. Open a Checking Account

Unless you're a sheepherder in Lower Mongolia, you need a checking account. Today, it's virtually impossible to get by without one. You can get by, but then you have to use money orders to pay at least some of your bills, and money orders are expensive — more expensive than checks.

But then, checking accounts can be expensive, too. First you have to pay for the checks, then you have to pay service fees each month. We all know about service fees, since most of us pay $5 or more a month to our bank so we can keep our checking account there. What's to be done?

What you can do is to cut out or reduce the service fees to the bank by shopping around. Perhaps you can get your checking account at a credit union that has no or low fees for checking accounts.

You should keep more than the minimum balance in your account. Form the habit of never dropping below the minimum balance, and always keep $100 or $200 above the minimum balance. Pick a figure, then stick to it.

2. Get Automatic Deposit

If you are like most people, you sell your labor for a paycheck. Do yourself a favor and have that paycheck deposited into your checking account automatically. It will save you time, and your time is valuable. In addition, you don't run the risk of losing or misplacing your paycheck.

3. Start an Emergency Fund

You need to start an emergency fund. You can have two emergency funds. The first emergency fund will be in a savings account so that it is handy. This emergency fund will be for small emergencies. You will pick a figure and you will save that amount of money in your savings account. Each time you withdraw money for a small emergency, you will immediately begin saving again until you have the desired amount of money in your savings account. Let's say you picked $1,000 for the figure in your first emergency fund. Once you save $1,000, stop putting money in that account. (Instead, you will be putting money into your second emergency fund.) If you have a car repair that costs $500 (perhaps that is your deductible), you will take $500 out of your savings account to pay for the car repair, and then you will save money again and keep depositing it into your savings account until you have $1,000.

The second emergency fund can be in a money market fund at a mutual fund such as Fidelity, T. Rowe Price, and Vanguard. This emergency fund will be for big emergencies. Again, you will pick a figure and you will save that amount of money. This time, however, you will keep saving. What is above the figure you picked out can be used for big-ticket items such a vacation. Let's say you picked $5,000 as your figure for your second emergency account. If the amount you have saved here reaches $7,000, you can feel free to take a $2,000 vacation or spend the $2,000 on whatever you want.

Of course, the $1,000 and the $5,000 figures are completely arbitrary. You will choose the figures that you think are right for you and your situation.

4. Start an IRA

Actually, you should do one more thing before you take that vacation: start an Individual Retirement Account. Set up an IRA at a mutual fund such as Fidelity, T. Rowe Price, and Vanguard.

The two types of IRAs are Traditional and Roth. With a Traditional IRA you may avoid paying income taxes on the money that you put into your IRA each year; however, you have to pay taxes on the money you withdraw from the IRA after you reach age 59 ½. You don't have to withdraw from your IRA until you reach 70 ½, but after that age you must withdraw a minimum amount of money per year.

With a Roth IRA, you pay taxes on the money you deposit into your IRA, but you do not have to pay taxes on the money you withdraw from the IRA after you reach age 59 ½. You don't have to withdraw from your IRA until you reach 70 ½, but after that age you must withdraw a minimum amount of money per year.

As of 2010, you may deposit $5,000 into your IRA each year, but if you are over age 50, you may deposit $6,000 into your IRA each year.

Other rules apply. I advise you to go to the Web site of a large mutual fund company such as Fidelity, T. Rowe Price, or Vanguard and research IRAs there.

IRAs are a good idea. Even if you have nothing but an IRA and an emergency account (plus, of course, a checking account), you will be doing better than many families in the United States.

This is my advice:

• Start an IRA early. Once you have an emergency fund, start an IRA as quickly as you can. The earlier you start an IRA, the longer the money has a chance to grow.

• Do not feel that you have to fully fund your IRA right away. The important thing is to set up with the minimum investment, and then to keep adding to it each month. If you can't afford to invest $5,000 per year right now, invest $1,000 or whatever you can afford each year. The main thing is to get started as quickly as possible. Each time you get a raise or more money, you can invest more in your IRA.

• Choose a mutual fund such as Vanguard that is known for its low costs to its investors. Other mutual funds have high fees that hurt their investors.

• Have money deposited into your IRA each month automatically. You can arrange to have money taken out of your checking account and sent to the mutual fund each month.

• How should you invest? Personal finance expert Scott Burns recommends what he calls a Couch Potato portfolio. A simple idea is to invest 50 percent in the Vanguard Total Stock Market Index fund and 50 percent in the Vanguard Total Bond Market Index fund. Once per year, you move money from one fund to the other so that once again you are 50 percent invested in each fund. The theory is that diversification (stocks and bonds) will help prevent very big losses. A person who is fully invested in stocks can have very big losses. A person who has 50 percent invested in bonds will suffer lesser losses because bonds are not as volatile (go up and down in value) as stocks. Be aware that some years you will lose money because some years are very bad years for the stock market.

Vanguard guru John Bogle recommends investing in both stocks and bonds. He recommends investing a percentage of your investment money corresponding to your age in the Vanguard Total Bond Index Fund, and the remaining percentage in the Vanguard Total Stock Market Index Fund. For example, if you are 30 years old, you will invest 30% of your mutual-fund money in the Vanguard Total Bond Index Fund and 70% of your mutual-fund money in the Vanguard Total Stock Market Index Fund. When you are 70, you will invest 70% of your mutual-fund money in the Vanguard Total Bond Index Fund and 30% of your mutual-fund money in the Vanguard Total Stock Market Index Fund. That way, your portfolio will become more conservative as you grow older.

By the way, index funds are different from actively managed funds. An index fund tries to match a benchmark. For example, an index fund may try to match the S&P 500 (500 large companies selected by Standard and Poor's to be representative of large companies. The managers of the index fund simply try to do as well as the S&P 500. In an actively managed fund, the managers of the fund try to do better than the benchmark — most fail to do that consistently.

Index funds tend to have lower costs than actively managed funds. It is very difficult to any manager to do better than the benchmark year after year.

5. Make Your Investing Automatic

I mentioned this briefly in the section above. You can arrange to have money automatically taken out of your checking account at a certain time each month and sent to a mutual fund such as Fidelity, T. Rowe Price, or Vanguard to be invested.

At your mutual fund company you may have both your big emergency fund and your IRA. Your big emergency fund may be a money market account on which you can write checks as long as they are for an amount of $250 or high. You may have two IRA accounts (perhaps the Vanguard Total Stock Market Index fund and the Vanguard Total Bond Market Index fund; other mutual fund companies have similar funds). You also should have your paycheck automatically deposited into your checking account each month. I recommend that you that you have money taken out of your checking account and sent to a mutual fund to be invested each month, perhaps a day or two after your paycheck is deposited.

You can easily go online and set this up after you have established an account at a mutual fund company. You can have a certain amount of money sent to your money market fund (your big emergency fund) and to your IRAs.

Each month you will live on the money that is left in your checking account after your monthly investments have been made.

This has many advantages:

• You are paying yourself first. You make your investments, and then you live on what's left. Paying yourself last does not work for most people. Some people think about investing the money that is left over at the end of the month, but seldom is any money left over.

• It is done automatically. All you have to remember to do is to go to your personal computer and put the transaction in your personal finance such as *Quicken*.

• The money will add up quickly over the months and years.

• With money in the bank and money in investments, you will feel better about yourself.

6. What to Do With Your Next Raise

It's easy for me to tell you to save so that you can establish your emergency fund, but you've got to do the hard work of actually saving the money so you can stash a few months' take-home pay somewhere safe so it's there when you need it — and to start an IRA. That can be tough.

I've given you one rule to follow so you can do it: Pay Yourself First. In following this rule, you take some money (at least ten percent) out of every check you get and save it even before you begin paying the bills. By saving it immediately, you form the habit of saving and soon learn that you can live as well or almost as well on ninety percent of your take-home salary as you used to live on all of it (eventually, you will live much better because you have saved ten percent of your take-home salary). Also, by saving it immediately, you don't notice that it's no longer there for you to spend. My next hint is related to this hint.

The next time you get a raise, save 50 percent of your raise each paycheck in addition to your normal ten percent of your take-home pay. You've managed to get along without the raise before; now you can manage to get along without spending the raise now. This method is a good way of increasing (without pain) the amount of your savings.

The same hint applies to the bonuses you may receive at Christmas or at other times. As soon as you get a bonus, earmark 50 percent of it immediately for savings. However, don't wait for a bonus to begin saving; always save ten percent of your take-home salary. It's the best habit you can make, and after making the habit, you start saving money automatically, without pain.

Of course, in the hard economic times of today, raises and bonuses for many people are nonexistent.

Chapter 4: How to Deal With Insurance and Other Evils

1. How Much Insurance Do You Need?

Insurance is widely viewed as a desirable thing, and it can be. Too often, however, it is not. The first thing you need to realize about insurance is that it should be used to protect yourself against very costly expenses, not against every expense that comes your (or your family's) way. Realizing that, we can start talking about the insurance you do (and the insurance you don't) need.

Life Insurance. First off, do you need life insurance? If you are young and single, you probably don't need it. Instead of paying the expense of insurance premiums, save and invest the money yourself. The purpose of life insurance is to protect the family you would leave behind if you die, so if you don't have a family, why bother with paying life insurance premiums? The only exception to this is when you want to leave an estate behind should you die tomorrow. If you are worried about what would happen to your parents or brothers and sisters when you die, you may choose to get life insurance. If that is the case, or if you are married, you should buy renewable term insurance, about which more in the second part of this chapter. Be aware that you don't need to get life insurance on your children. Children tend not to be wage earners, and you probably don't have to worry about replacing their income when they die.

Car Insurance. Next, if you have a car, you definitely need liability insurance. Liability insurance is necessary insurance. If you cause an accident and seriously harm someone, you could be liable for large sums of money — the kind you can't go to your savings account to get. This is the kind of situation that good insurance is designed to cover. Get plenty of liability insurance.

You may or may not want insurance to cover your own car. If you drive a clunker, don't bother (but be sure to get liability insurance). Simply put the money that would have gone to the insurance company into a savings account. If you have an accident, take the money out of your savings account and replace your clunker. As long as you can replace fairly easily what's lost, you don't need insurance.

If you have a new car or one you could not easily replace if it should get totaled, then you should have insurance on it. Get the highest deductible you can to save on insurance premiums. Your insurance will help you out if your car is totaled, but you won't be spending a fortune on premiums.

Two more tips about cars and car insurance. First, shop around to find out what kind of deal you can get on premiums. Be sure to check out a few places and compare their rates. Second, drive defensively and carefully. If you die in a car accident, it won't be much comfort to you that your car is insured.

Fire Insurance. If you have a house, you definitely need fire insurance. You may want to insure everything in your home for its replacement value, not for its actual value. If your stereo burns in a fire, you want to be able to replace it. Otherwise, if your $1,000 stereo burns in a fire, you may only get $800 for it (because of depreciation before the fire), although it may cost you $1200 to replace it at today's prices.

Tenants Insurance. If you rent, it is a god idea to have tenants insurance, both to replace property in case of a fire and to protect in cases of liability if someone were to fall on your stairs.

Health Insurance. Another essential is health insurance. One kind of expense you ordinarily can't handle by yourself is that resulting from a long illness. Be sure to shop around, and get the highest deductible you can to save on premiums. And hope to have a job that provides good health insurance.

Disability Insurance. If you are young, you are much more likely to become disabled than you are to die. Becoming disabled either temporarily or permanently will be very expensive, so disability insurance can take some of the financial sting out of being disabled. Be forewarned: disability insurance is expensive and most insurers will not cover 100 percent of your salary (they want it to be to your advantage to get back to work). Be sure to compare policies and to check out each insurance company's definition of "disability" very carefully. You probably will want to get disability insurance that covers you if you can't work at the job you now hold. Some policies won't pay you if, for example, you are injured and can't work at your usual job, but are not so injured that you can't hold down a job at McDonald's for a much smaller salary.

Many kinds of insurance you do not need. You don't need flight insurance or any other kind of insurance that covers one type of accident or one type of illness. Instead, make your health insurance comprehensive.

2. Renewable Term Life Insurance

If you really do need life insurance, then you should get renewable life insurance. Stay away from whole-life insurance and its variations — or check them out carefully. These are insurance-with-savings programs; however, usually they are expensive and the savings portion of the plan ineffective. The situation bears watching, but probably you can do much better by paying for renewable term insurance and banking the difference in your own savings plan. With term insurance, all you get is insurance. If you have a $100,000 term life insurance policy and you die while you're covered, your beneficiary will get $100,000. It's as simple as that. Renewable simply means that you can renew it year after year.

3. Take Care of Your Body

The people I'm writing this small book for aren't millionaires who can live off investment income. Instead, they're people who will work for salary or perhaps will start a small business of their own. As such, much of the money they will make will come from their own labor.

Because of this, one of the best investments they — and you, and I — can make is to take care of our bodies. An illness or accident — even if we have disability insurance — can take away much of our income (and happiness), so we need to practice preventive medicine by taking care of our bodies. Exercising, watching our diets, paying attention to symptoms, getting annual dental and medical checkups — all these can play a role in keeping us whole both in health and in finances.

And, of course, pay attention to these rules:

- Drive defensively.
- Wear your seatbelt.
- Don't smoke.
- Avoid dangerous illegal drugs.
- If you drink, drink moderately.
- Eat your fruits and vegetables.
- Eat whole grains.
- Avoid trans fats.
- Maintain a healthy weight.
- Exercise regularly.
- Enjoy life.
- Maintain good relations with family and friends.
- Avoid doing evil.
- Do good.
- Pay attention to the spiritual side of life.

Chapter 5: How to Invest Your Money

1. Diversify

Perhaps the most important rule in investing is to diversify. This rule is based on no more deep thought than the cliché "Don't keep all your eggs in one basket." If you put all your eggs in one basket and you drop the basket, then all your eggs will break. If you put all your investment money in one investment and that investment crashes, then so does all your investment money.

Even before you begin to invest (if you are following my financial program), you should have some diversification because some of your savings are in cash (savings and checking accounts, money market accounts) or cash equivalents (Certificates of Deposit, aka CDs, which are available at banks and credit unions). By now, of course, you've started your checking account and have stashed your small emergency fund in a safe place, such as a FDIC-insured bank. In the next step of your financial plan, you need to make sure that you don't put all your investment money into one basket.

If you also have your big emergency fund in a money market account at a mutual fund such as Fidelity, T. Rowe Price, or Vanguard and if you have two IRAs (one invested in stocks, and the other invested in bonds), you are diversified. If you also have a house, you are further diversified.

Read further for a basic understanding of a few basic investments.

2. Mutual Funds

Mutual funds are run by professionals for anyone, including the public, who chooses to invest with them. In a mutual fund several people — perhaps several hundred thousand investors — pool their money together so that the professionals who run the fund can invest it for them.

Mutual funds come in several types. Many invest their funds in stocks; others concentrate on bonds; others are money-market mutual funds. The similarity of all these mutual funds is that investors pool their money so that a professional can invest it.

Often, mutual funds come in families. This means that you can choose from and invest in several mutual funds. One may be a money-market mutual fund; one may be for bonds; another may be for equities. Equities are stocks — a share of stock is simply one portion of ownership in a company. As you can imagine, large corporations are divided into many millions of shares of ownership.

This arrangement has several advantages for the investors. First, the investor with little money to invest has immediate diversification. Let's say that the investor wishes to invest in stocks. Instead of buying a few shares in just one company on the New York Stock Exchange, the investor buys a few shares in a mutual fund that has its assets invested in many stocks on the New York Stock Exchange (and perhaps other exchanges, as well).

For extra diversification, invest in a family of mutual funds as your savings increase. Start with a money-market mutual fund (for your big emergency fund), and then invest in an equity (stock) mutual fund, and in a bond mutual fund. Since you now have diversification, sit back, send in money regularly, and watch your net worth increase over time (knowing that, unfortunately, in some years the mutual fund(s) may go down in value).

As owners of shares in a mutual fund, we can relax and let the professionals do the work for us. Instead of our spending hours each week reading the *Wall Street Journal* and other financial publications, we can simply go online once in a while to see how our mutual funds are doing.

Since we don't have to spend hours each week studying the stock and bond markets, we can concentrate on professional development in our own jobs. Let the professionals do their job; that'll let us do ours.

Our mutual fund will do a lot of our record keeping for us. Usually, we'll receive a statement each quarter of every year, and for tax purposes, a statement by Jan. 31 of every year. The statement will tell us how much we've made in interest or in dividends, as well as how much we've invested in the mutual fund. Our record keeping is limited mostly to filing away the statements we receive from our mutual fund.

Another advantage is that costs can be kept to a minimum, especially if you choose a no-load fund to invest in.

3. Make Your Mutual Fund No Load

The kind of mutual fund I've been writing about, and that I recommend the small investor invest in, is open end. This means that the number of shares in the mutual fund varies day to day. If lots of people want to invest in the mutual fund, the fund will sell them new shares. If lots of people want to get out of the mutual fund, the fund will redeem (buy back) their shares. So the number of shares of the fund varies from day to day.

This is opposed to the closed-end fund, which has a fixed number of shares and which is traded on a stock exchange. You can buy shares in open-end funds directly from the fund, thus avoiding the brokerage fee you have to pay if you bought directly from a broker.

The kind of open-end mutual fund I recommend that you invest in is no-load. If your fund has a load, that means that there's a sales charge — which can be four percent, or eight percent, or more! — each time you buy (and sometimes each time you sell) shares in your mutual fund. Who needs that!

Whatever mutual fund you choose, make it no-load.

4. Re-Invest Your Dividends or Interest

When you invest in a mutual fund, you can make money in two ways: dividends or interest, and capital appreciation. Your capital will appreciate (increase) when the stocks your equity mutual fund invests in sell for more than when it bought them, or when the bonds your bond mutual fund invests in sell for more than when it bought them. When that happens, great. (Sometimes, your capital will decrease.)

Since we're talking in this book about increasing your net worth, let it keep on happening. Keep investing money in your mutual fund.

One way to continue to invest in your mutual fund is to re-invest all dividends and interest in your mutual funds. A dividend is money that a company's board of directors votes to send to its stockholders. If your mutual fund owns 100 shares of Company XYZ, and the board of directors of Company XYZ votes an annual dividend of $1, then you will receive $100 (paid in four quarterly installments of $25). Interest is the money you earn from holding bonds. Whatever dividends or interest your mutual fund earns, it's a good idea to re-invest them.

When you start an account with a mutual fund, that mutual fund will ask if you want to reinvest your dividends and/or your interest. Tell your mutual funds to reinvest your dividends and interest. That way, small sums (which over the years will turn into larger and larger sums) get invested and start working for you. This is a painless way of investing — and one you should not ignore.

5. Dollar-Cost Averaging

Dollar-cost averaging is another good idea that the small investor can take advantage of. A small investor can invest a certain amount of money in his or her mutual fund each month, month after month, year after year. By doing so, the investor buys fewer shares of stock when share prices are high, more shares of stock when share prices are low. The advantage of this is that the investor doesn't have to worry about timing the market — that is, trying to guess when the market is low so the investor can buy shares of stock at low prices. Instead, the small investor simply invests the same amount of money month after month, year after year. When you get a promotion, increase the amount of money you send in to be invested. And, of course, have money automatically taken from your checking account to be automatically invested each month.

6. Investigate Before You Invest

Another very important rule in investing is to investigate before you invest. A lot of people out there would love to have your investment dollars. Some of those people are honest; some are not. To tell the difference, you have to investigate; that investigation should come before you hand over your money. Remember, if an investment sounds too good to be true, it probably is.

Many investments, such as mutual funds, are accompanied are prospectuses, which are booklets that state the rules you must follow to invest in the mutual fund and to redeem your shares. The prospectus also gives you a lot of information that you can use to determine whether that mutual fund would make a good investment for you. It will give such information as this:

1) the philosophy of the fund: whether it's most interested in growth, maximum growth, income, or whatever. Of course, when it comes to stocks and bonds, I recommend index funds.

2) the expenses of the fund. Some funds have higher expenses than others — guess who pays the expenses.

3) the past returns of the fund. Of course, past performance is no guarantee of the future performance of the fund.

7. The Fancy Stuff: Avoid It

The best thing I can tell you about the fancy stuff is to avoid it. As a small investor, the fanciest thing you need to invest in is an Individual Retirement Account (IRA), which can be called the poor man's tax shelter. If you should ever get a call about investing in gold mines, or fancy tax shelters, or penny stocks, or new issues, or whatever, hang up. The better the deal sounds, and the more "guarantees" the promoter gives you, the faster you should hang up.

Remember: If a deal sounds too good to be true, it probably is excellent for the promoter, but not at all good for you.

A good rule to follow is to understand something before you invest in it. I have written about investing in mutual funds, but before you invest in one, you should write for its prospectus and read it carefully.

Chapter 6: How to Prepare for Retirement

1. The Three Legs of Retirement

Usually, three legs support your retirement. The first of these is Social Security; next comes your Individual Retirement Account and other investments; last is your pension. None of these by themselves may be enough to support you in retirement, but all three of them together can lead to a happy and prosperous retirement. Unfortunately, pensions seem to be becoming fewer in number, so if you can, save and invest more money.

Although you may be only in your 20s or 30s, now is the time to start planning your retirement. After all, someday you hope to be well off (or you wouldn't be reading this), and someday you hope to retire (dying an early death may be romantic in the movies but is hardly satisfactory in real life). Begin planning now so that your net worth increases each year and so that in retirement you won't have to worry about money.

2. Social Security

Social Security is something you have probably been paying into since you began working. It is something you have earned, not something you are being given by the government. Our government has made us fork over some of our hard-earned cash each time we receive a pay check, and in return it has promised to give us a check each month after we retire until we die.

Despite the noises government officials and others are making about Social Security being in a hole when the baby boomers finally start retiring in great numbers, we can assume that we will get something when we retire. Otherwise, the government would probably not survive the resulting loss of its credibility. (Vote the rascals out! And televise the revolution!) Believe me, politicians are well aware that old people vote. We can also assume that what we receive from Social Security will not be enough to support ourselves well.

3. IRAs and Other Individual Plans

You really don't have much control over Social Security; the government makes all the decisions concerning that. However, you do have control over your Individual Retirement Account (IRA) and other personal investments and savings. Here is one place you can help ensure that you will have a comfortable retirement.

An IRA is an account that you can set up today so that you can withdraw money from it after retirement. The first essential of an IRA is that it really is money for retirement, so you would invest money in it that you won't need until retirement. The other essential to realize is that since you do intend to retire someday you should open an IRA today. If you have a 10-20-70 budget (10 percent of take-home pay is kept in long-term savings; 20 percent in savings for big-ticket items such as a house, a car, or a computer (or to pay off debt); and 70 percent for living expenses), then an IRA is a good place to keep at least some of that 10 percent of take-home pay that you reserve for long-term (not to be touched until retirement) savings.

Opening an IRA account is easy and can be done in many different places. You can open your IRA account at either a bank or a credit union. At either place the form for opening an IRA account is easy to fill out. If you open your IRA at a bank, you would probably invest in CDs.

I recommend that you open your IRA at a mutual fund such as Fidelity, T. Rowe Price, or Vanguard. If you open your IRA at a mutual fund, you may choose two mutual funds to invest in and decide the percentage of your IRA money you want to invest in each one. I have recommended a broadly based stock fund and a broadly based bond fund, with 50 percent invested in each.

In general, you will try to save as much as possible in your IRA so as to have it when you retire. You may have a good reason not to invest the maximum amount of money in an IRA; however, there are not as many good reasons as a heavy spender might expect. If you are saving for the down payment on a house, you may not want to contribute the maximum amount of money to your IRA. Since your own house would be a major asset and since it would greatly contribute to your quality of life, for many people it is a wise move to buy your own house.

However, even if you are planning to save the down payment to buy your own house, I recommend that you start an IRA for the simple reason that getting started is the hardest thing to do. What you may wish to do is to start your IRA, contribute to it a small amount each month at the same time you are saving up to buy a house. After buying the house, immediately start contributing more money to your IRA.

Your IRA is just part of the money you can invest for your retirement. If you own your home, it is a major asset that may appreciate in value. Other savings and investments mean that you will have more money in retirement. Still, because of its tax-advantaged status, an IRA is an investment that can reduce your tax bill now and grow for the future.

The age at which you start your IRA and the percentage return you get affect the amount you will eventually have in your IRA. One point is obvious: The earlier you start investing, the longer the time your money has to grow.

In building up your IRA, compound interest works wonders. The money you invest makes interest, then that interest make interest, then the interest that the interest made makes interest, etc.

4. Pension

Your pension is another leg of your retirement. Many of us will work years for a company, the government, or a school system, and will receive a pension when we retire. Your pension fund managers should give you an accounting each year, letting you know how much you have invested in the pension fund. Get information about this at your place of employment.

5. Putting It All Together

So, the three legs of retirement are Social Security, your IRA and other personal savings and investments, and your pension. All three of these will work together to support you in retirement. Normally, you will receive checks from Social Security and from your pension fund, and you can withdraw money as needed from your IRA. If your IRA is invested at a mutual fund, you can have the mutual fund send you a check each month.

One advantage that you will have when you retire is that your expenses should decrease, thus making living on a smaller annual income easier. A disadvantage is that as you grow older, your medical expenses will probably increase.

In retirement, your only concerns won't be financial, although financial concerns are the focus of this book. You will need a reason to get up in the morning. That reason can come from hobbies, volunteering, whatever. Practice an art now, and continue to practice it when you retire. Chances are, you want to do more in retirement than watch TV. One important recommendation I can make is for you to make taking care of your body a priority when you retire — and now. (This is an important recommendation for me, too.)

Getting your finances together is only one thing you need to do to get ready for retirement.

Chapter 7: How to Spend Your Money

1. The Advantage of Having Money

Ever notice how those who have always seem to be able to get more? It definitely seems that those who have, get more, while those who don't have, never get at all. There is a lot of truth in this. As country singer Roy Clark says, if you don't have a nickel to your name and suddenly boats are on sale for five cents each, all you'll be able to do is to run up and down the bank and shout, "Ain't that cheap!" Meanwhile, the people with the money are buying the bargains.

One major reason that you need money is so that you've got money when things are on sale. Otherwise, you'll have to buy things when you need them, whether they're on sale or not. A person with money in the bank can buy winter gloves, hats, and coats when they're on sale early in the spring; a person without money in the bank has to buy them when they're needed, whether they're on sale or not.

2. A Well-Stocked Larder

One of the advantages of having money is having a well-stocked larder. When things are on sale, buy more of them than you need. Fill your kitchen or storage room with canned food (bought on sale), paper goods (bought on sale), and items that are used every day (be sure to buy them on sale).

The advantages of doing this are many:

• You've saved money by buying on sale.

• You'll have a nice feeling of security that comes from having a storage room stocked with things you need.

• You won't run out of the items you keep stored.

• You won't need to run to the store as often to get something essential.

• You won't be affected by inflation so much since the stuff that's stored was bought at yesterday's (sale) prices.

• You won't need to dip into savings to buy food at the end of the month if your larder is well stocked with food bought on sale.

• If there's ever a natural (or man-caused) disaster in your area, you'll be better prepared than many of your neighbors.

3. Houses, Cars, and Other Big-Ticket Items

Some things we most want (and often most need) also cost the most. "Big-ticket" items such as buying a house, car, or perhaps a home computer fall into that category. Buying these items takes special preparation.

Arranging a 10-20-70 budget is a good way to prepare for buying these high-priced items. With this budget, 10 percent of your take-home goes into long-term savings, 20 percent is used to save up for big-ticket items such as the down payment for a house, and 70 percent is used for living expenses.

The 10-20-70 budget is a good way to manage your budget at all times. The 20 percent of your budget that you save for the big-ticket items mounts up quickly, and soon you will be able to make a substantial down payment on or buy outright that big-ticket item you've set your eyes on.

4. Saving on Mortgages

A big-ticket item almost everyone has his or her eyes set on, but hardly anyone can afford to buy outright, is a house. A mortgage is a necessity for most people who want t own a house. Here are two ways to save on your mortgage:

1) If you are able, get a 15-year mortgage instead of a 30-year mortgage. True, your monthly payments will be higher, but the money you save on interest will be greatly significant. Why pay the bank for 30 years when you can pay for only 15 years? By taking out a 15-year mortgage instead of taking out a 30-year mortgage, you will own your home 15 years earlier, your equity will build up much more quickly, and you will save a fortune in interest payments.

2) Set up your mortgage so that your bank doesn't charge a penalty for your paying off your mortgage early. Then send in additional money each time (or as often as you can) you make a mortgage payment. Along with the extra money, send the bank a note saying that the money is to be applied to the principal (not the interest) of your loan. Be aware, however, that although you send in extra money one month, you still need to make your usual mortgage payment every month.

Chapter 8: How to Give to Charity

1. Peter Singer's Argument to Assist

Should we give money to charity?

Most people would probably answer yes, but other than giving a few coins when someone waves a canister under their nose, do not in fact give to charity.

The philosopher Peter Singer, however, would argue that we have a moral obligation to give money to charity.

In his book *Practical Ethics*, Singer bases his argument on the premise that "if we can prevent something bad without sacrificing anything of comparable moral significance, we ought to do it." He uses this premise to argue that we ought to give money to poor people in undeveloped countries. His basic argument, however, can be used to show that we ought to give money to many other charities.

Singer argues that, since absolute poverty — that is, poverty by any standard — is bad, and since there is some absolute poverty that we can prevent without sacrificing anything of comparable moral significance, we ought to prevent some absolute poverty.

No one would argue that absolute poverty is bad. We have all seen photographs of starving families in third-world countries. We would agree that no child ought to go to bed hungry, and we find it horrifying that in some parts of the world half of all children will die before they reach the age of five.

More controversial is Singer's premise that we can prevent some absolute poverty. We have all read of inefficient or corrupt charities that collect money for a worthy cause, but somehow, only a fraction of the money collected gets into the hands of the people who need it. The rest of the money goes for "expenses," more fundraising or even parties. We also have read of corrupt governments that take the money collected for their people and instead put it in private Swiss bank accounts or buy weapons with it.

Still, some organizations seem to be efficient and to address the needs of the absolutely poor. These programs show that some absolute poverty can be prevented. If we agree with Singer's argument, then we should work to prevent some absolute poverty.

Singer leaves it to us to determine how much we ought to give. Most Americans have enough food, clothing and shelter, as well as money left over for luxuries such as a color television or a second car.

The basic form of Singer's argument can also be used to show that we ought to try to prevent other bad things from happening. Absolute poverty is bad, but so is rape. Some absolute poverty is preventable; with rape prevention programs, some rapes can be prevented. So we can conclude that we ought to prevent some rapes and we ought to help the survivors of rape. Chances are, your community has a rape crisis center. It deserves to be supported.

Many other things are bad, but can be alleviated. When we can, we should alleviate them.

Giving to charity is in many ways an act of faith. The person who gives to charity has faith that his or her gift will make the world a better place to live than before he or she gave the gift. In many cases, they are right.

2. Investigate Before You Give

In a way, giving to charity can be regarded as an investment. It's an expense in financial terms, of course, but still you can regard the money you spend as an investment in the future of the world. There are many places to give your money, but no matter to whom or to which charity you give your money, you are trying to make the world a little better — both now and in the future.

In your financial life, you will probably both be investing for a personal return of wealth for yourself and giving to charity as a way to invest in a better world for all. Some of the same rules apply to both kinds of investments.

The most important of these rules is this: Investigate Before You Give. Yes, you are giving your money away, but still, you want to give wisely, just as you want to invest wisely. So you need to become familiar with the charities to which — if they deserve it — you will give some of your money.

Sometimes judging charities can be difficult. Much of the money raised by Mothers Against Drunk Driving (MADD) goes toward sending out fund-funding letters, but one can argue, as financial writer Andrew Tobias does, that these letters are a forum to educate the public about the dangers that drunk drivers pose.

Investigating charities before you give money to them is an unfortunate necessity simply because some charities are inefficient and others are outright frauds.

3. Diversify

I recommend a certain amount of diversification in your charitable donations. For one thing, you may find out later that one charity has been less efficient than it should be. If you diversify, you will avoid giving all of your charity dollars to an inefficient charity. However, I also recommend diversification because there are so many worthwhile causes to support, so many worthwhile battles to fight.

Diversify, if possible. The first kind of diversification is to donate to more than one charity, the second is to give to both local and national or international charities, and the third is to give to both the kinds of charities that serve to help humankind to survive and to the kinds that serve to uplift humankind through the arts.

You may not want that much diversification. No problem. It's your money. Give it to whichever charity or charities you want.

A final word: One of the pleasures of having money is being able to help other people. If you read about a tragedy in your newspaper and read that money is being collected for the people who suffered the tragedy, you can do a couple of things. One, you can say, "Isn't that awful," then turn to the comic page. Two, you can reach for your checkbook and send some money where it can do some good.

4. Limit Your Diversification

Still, when giving to charities, you don't want to spread your donations too thin. You'll find your mailbox full of solicitations, and those letters cost the charity money. Instead, investigate a few charities and then stick with them. If you ignore the other charities, they'll stop sending solicitations to you and spend that money better elsewhere (we hope!).

If you donate money to a national or international charity, you will find your mailbox full of solicitations. Charities often share lists of donators. If you give money to each charity, you will have to be very rich, indeed. In my opinion, it's better to give more dollars to fewer charities than to give fewer dollars to more charities. I want my money to go to people who need it; I don't want it to be spent on sending out form letters.

5. Know When Not to Give

There is a time not to give as well as a time to give. Much of the money we Americans give to charity is given when someone waves a canister under our noses. This is usually not a good time to give, even if all we give is pocket change. There is no time to investigate the charity and no way to tell if the money gets to where you intended it to go. This is a field for thieves.

Of course, exceptions exist. If the street is filled with kids wearing band uniforms and they say they are collecting for their high school band, it's a reasonable assumption that they are telling the truth. The Salvation Army Christmas kettles are well known, too, and the Salvation Army is an efficient charity.

But, in general, keep your change in your pockets; when you donate, write a check and send it directly to the charity — avoid the middleperson.

Also, be aware of what are known as "guilt gifts." Often, a charity will send you a fund-raising letter and a guilt gift — a trinket such as a key ring or something such as address labels. The purposes for doing that are to get you to open the envelope and to make you feel as if you have to give money to such a nice charity. I don't like guilt gifts, and I don't give money to charities that send me guilt gifts. I want the charity to spend money on people who need it, not spend money to send me a key ring — I already have a key ring.

If a charity sends you guilt gifts, I recommend writing the charity and asking it to take you off its mailing list. A charity once sent me a dime — and spent money on postage to do so. I wish that all of the dimes that the charity had sent to contributors (and all of the money spent on postage) had gone to the people that the charity was supposed to be helping.

6. Charity Begins at Home

Another good use of money is simply to take care of your own. You don't want your family to have to rely on charity, so help take care of them. If you want to, spend your money on gifts that you know that the old folks (or the young folks) in your family will use and appreciate.

And, of course, you may want to support your church or synagogue.

Chapter 9: Free Advice

1. Form good habits.

You decide which good habits you want to form. Some of them will be things that you ought to do and so you form a habit of doing them so that you do them automatically.

Other habits may be such things as reading every day. It's up to you.

2. Do not form bad habits.

Avoid forming the habit of over-eating, and avoid forming the habit of under-exercising, and you won't have to worry about becoming obese.

Avoid the habit of smoking, and you increase your chances of living a long, healthy life.

Avoid addiction to illegal drugs, and you can save yourself a heaping helping of trouble.

And so on.

3. Divide actions into three groups: 1) actions you have to do, 2) actions you ought to do, and 3) actions you want to do.

Try to be efficient at doing the actions you have to do. They usually include making a living for adults, and studying for students. Try to find ways to do them well, and perhaps quickly. For studying, you may want to form the habit of studying at a certain time and place. In some families, once the dishes are washed and dried after the evening meal, the kids sit down at the dinner table and do homework until the homework is done.

Try to make habits of the things you ought to do. Make a habit of eating one or more veggies at every meal. Make a habit of flossing in the morning and in the evening. Make a habit of stretching when you wake up in the morning (or some other habitual time). If they become habits, you will do them automatically.

If the things you want to do don't conflict with the things you have to do and the things you ought to do, go ahead and do them. If you are an adult and you want to read fairy stories, go ahead and read fairy stories.

4. Live a Life of Wit and Intelligence

Because why wouldn't you?

Conclusion

Everyone wants to live well instead of just living. Just living can mean living from paycheck to paycheck, always needing something and always having to spend your paycheck because of your many needs. It can mean being afraid of financial emergencies — even minor ones. By following the program set out here, you can alleviate that situation.

If you follow the steps outlined above — budget, know your net worth, pay yourself first, save and invest — the financial part of your life should soon be under control, but of course that's just one part of your life. In addition, you should realize that having control of your financial life doesn't mean that you can buy anything you want.

Actually, it's the people who try to buy anything they want who run into trouble because of huge credit card bills. They try to have it all and end up having little or nothing. No wonder; after all, how much is enough? No matter what you have, it's easy to want more (and often to *need* more).

However, with the program outlined here, you should be able to have the things that are the most important to you, even if it means having to save for them. The real meaning of security doesn't mean having everything you've ever wanted; instead, you will be more financially secure by having money in the bank, a well-stocked larder, an emergency fund in a safe place, and most important, being in control of your finances.

Following the advice in this document won't make anyone rich, but it should help many people achieve at least some of their goals (assuming that not all of your goals are things such as this: being invisible). Some risk is involved, but the advice should be sound. You, of course, will have to decide whether to use this advice. You certainly don't have to invest in a mutual fund at Fidelity, T. Rowe Price, Vanguard, or anywhere else. And, of course, I am not responsible for any losses that a mutual fund or other investment may suffer. You make your own investment decisions, and you have the responsibility for them.

Of course, other things are important: being with family, loving other people, enjoying the arts, life, and work, and taking care of your body and mind. Not being overly stressed about money can help you to enjoy those other things more.

A Small, Select Bibliography

Clason, George S. *The Richest Man in Babylon*. New York: Bantam Books, 1955. Written in parables, this book contains much excellent advice.

Thoreau, Henry David. *Walden*. Read especially the first chapter, titled "Economy."

Tobias, Andrew. *Money Angles*. New York: Avon Books, 1984. Tobias is both intelligent and funny. His books about money make sense for the small investor. Some of them are divided into two parts: The first part deals with financial basics which everyone, including the small investor, should know, while the second part details Tobias' adventures (and misadventures) in the financial markets. We, of course, should avoid the fancy stuff. However, we can enjoy Andrew Tobias' adventures (and misadventures) when he engages in the fancy stuff.

Tobias, Andrew. *Still! The Only Investment Guide You'll Ever Need*. New York: Bantam Books. Updated every few years.

Down and Out in Athens, Ohio
Chapter 1: My Life and Hard Times

I have been single all my life so far, and I expect to be single for the rest of my life. I like being alone. I know men who go hunting not because they like to hunt, but because it is the only time all year they can be alone for more than a few minutes. I am the type of person who likes to be alone for most of each day. I can visit family on vacation and be around people for most of a few days, but then I need to get back home so I can be alone.

Quite simply, I am the type of man who finds the life led by Jack Nicholson's character in *As Good as It Gets* to be quite attractive, except for the misogyny, and the racism, and the cowardice, and the obsessive-compulsive disorder, and probably a few other things. Still, he makes a good living by writing novels and he spends much of each day alone. Then he had to go and ruin it all by falling in love. (It's hard to believe that I have a sister — Brenda Kennedy — who writes romance books.)

To any women who write complaining posts on Reddit's Forever Alone thread, I apologize. I also give you permission to say that you and I used to be engaged to be married, but we called off the wedding due to a matter of life and death — we would have killed each other. You might be able to use this story to answer prying questions about why you haven't married or remarried yet. Add all the gruesome details you want. Be sure to blame me.

But I do have children, just not biological children. As a teacher at Ohio University in Athens, Ohio, which is commonly confused with Ohio State University in Columbus, Ohio, I taught 60 or more adult children — usually from age 18 to 22 (Yay! No poopy diapers!) — each quarter, back when Ohio University was on the quarter system.

Most of my students were angels, but some were not. Unfortunately, I found plagiarism in student papers and in some cases I sent the student to University Judiciaries, where the most common punishment dealt to guilty students was being put on Academic Probation. Even more unfortunately, I am positive that I did not discover all the plagiarism that occurred. Most students, of course, worked hard and did not plagiarize.

Here's an example of academic dishonesty that was not committed by one of my students, but that one of my students told me about. My student and her acquaintance were taking a class in computer programming, but both were having a hard time learning the subject. When the final computer-programming project was due, neither had been able to complete it, but another student gave copies of his work to everyone who wanted it. My student was honest and did not pass off work as her own that she had not done. Her acquaintance, however, accepted a copy of the other student's work and handed it in as her own work. Result: My student failed with an F, and her acquaintance passed with an A. My student retook the class, learned how to program, put the class on her resume, and got a job as a computer programmer. Her acquaintance did not retake the class, did not learn how to program, put the class on her resume, and got a job as a computer programmer. My student was a good programmer and kept her job, while her acquaintance was not a good programmer and got fired. My student then made a Xerox copy of her paycheck and mailed it to her acquaintance with this note: "Ha! Ha!"

Among any group of people, of course, most members of the group will be angels and a few will be devils. Usually, one student will be high-maintenance and ask for special privileges such as handing in papers late without penalty or missing many classes without penalty. Let's face it, not everyone is competent. Some people can't work well on their own, or with others, and their supervisors sometimes feel such people can't walk unless the supervisor tells them which foot to use to take the first step.

Here's an example of one of the students who failed one of my classes. The student missed my class one day, and so he sent me an email giving an explanation of why he missed my class: His alarm clock didn't go off. Hmm, the class met at noon!

Of course, sometimes students have better excuses for missing class. One student met with me before class started and asked to be excused because she fell nauseous after another class during which her professor had dissected a human leg. I excused her, but I also said that in a future year the leg being dissected might be mine because I have donated my body to the Ohio University Heritage College of Osteopathic Medicine.

One student wrote this memorable evaluation at the end of one quarter: "If I ever have just one hour left to live, I hope that I spend it in David Bruce's class." Of course, I felt pretty good reading this, but then I read the next sentence: "One hour in David Bruce's class lasts forever."

Some of my students had email addresses other than their email address at Ohio University. Once in a while, a student would have as their email address drunkguy111@hotmailcom or partygirl111@gmail.com. Let's hope that they don't use these email addresses on their resumes.

Of course, any student can make mistakes. A student once sent me an email that began, "Hell, Bruce." No, he wasn't angry at me; he simply didn't proofread. He had meant to write, "Hello, Bruce."

Also, of course, you don't have to be a student to make a mistake. Channel 4 (Columbus, Ohio) News once gave a quiz to help determine if you are a hypochondriac. After giving the quiz, the news co-anchor, Colleen Marshall, said, "If you think you are a hypochondriac, you should see a doctor."

By the way, Columbus, Ohio, radio deejay Bob Simpson once asked listeners for silly pet names. One caller had a friend who had named his cat "Stir Fry." Why? "It's a threat."

Back when I was a student at Ohio University, my roommate and his best friend wanted to go on Spring Break in Florida, but they had hardly any money, and certainly not enough money for food. They ended up stealing apples and brownies from the cafeteria. (Students were not allowed to take cafeteria food back to the dorms.) Of course, the brownies grew hard and stale, and they grew tired of eating apples, so they stole food from stores. They would go in a store, unwrap an ice cream sandwich, shove half of it in their mouth when no one was looking and then shove the other half in their mouth when no one was looking. God, of course, was looking, and God punished them with incredibly painful brain-freeze.

By the way, one of the students in my dorm had no morning classes, and so he slept late. However, his student meal card included breakfast, and so he would set his alarm, go to the cafeteria in his pajamas, bathrobe, and slippers, eat breakfast, and then go back to his room and sleep.

Also by the way, Ohio University frequently hosts such special occasions as Moms Weekend, during which students' mothers come to visit them. I once got a big laugh at the beginning of a class by saying after one Moms Weekend, "I must be getting old. Some of these OU moms look hot!"

The angels among my students made me marvel at their work. I frequently taught freshman and junior composition and technical writing, and I attempted to make the writing my students did useful. I would assign the writing of a 10- to 20-page manual in many classes, but I would allow students to write more pages and many students responded with 60-page manuals. Why? They got into the project and knew that it would help them. They were writing for themselves, not just for a grade, which is the way it should be.

Two of my students who had studied in France as part of the Ohio University Study Abroad Program worked together on a manual for students who would be in that program. Jobs in France opened up that were associated with the Study Abroad Program, and both students applied for those jobs and both submitted copies of the manual they had co-written. One student was given a job immediately. The other student was officially a little too young, but she got the job after a slight delay. Why did she get the job? She got it because of the manual she had co-written for my class. In fact, the person who hired her was flipping through the manual and looking at and reading it as he talked to my student on the phone to tell her she had the job. These two students got paid to live in France. Nice!

Another student wrote a 60-page employee manual for the job he did working for the Ohio University football team. He was responsible for such tasks as getting things ready for game day. He was in Sports Sciences, and he ended up getting a very competitive job internship because he sent the sports organization a copy of the manual he wrote for my class.

Michelle Griesmer wrote a huge manual about how to be a lighting director. She worked professionally one summer on a TV program and was excited to get a copy of the program. Of course, she looked for her name in the credits; unfortunately, she was listed as *Michael* Griesmer.

Another student did a long problem-solving manual for the company she worked for. She identified problems at the company and made recommendations about how to solve those problems. She was given a $1,000 bonus for writing the problem-solving manual.

In my composition classes, I always had the assignment of writing a problem-solving letter in which students identify one or more problems and make recommendations about how to solve it or them. I have had students actually mail the letters, which was optional in my class. At least one student received the offer of a promotion and a raise to come back after graduation and work at that company. (She turned the company down because she had a better offer.)

One of my favorite assignments in some of my composition classes was the autobiographical essay, which focused mainly on funny incidents in my students' lives. I well remember many of those essays. For example, Maggie Wendell wrote about the first day of her first class as a freshman at Ohio University. It was a public-speaking class, and she was shocked when she learned that the professor was going to have the students speak for five minutes without preparation on a topic that the professor would tell them. Maggie is a student who likes to be super-prepared for every test and every assignment, so impromptu speaking is not at all her thing. When it was her turn and she got her topic, she immediately began staring at the back wall and spewing whatever verbal diarrhea came into her mind. She even invented an Asian-American friend as she talked about the *youth in Asia*. When her five minutes was up, she stopped talking and saw that the other students were looking at her and trying to stifle laughter. What was wrong? Were her pants unzipped? Her professor said, "Thank you, Ms. Wendell, for your enlightening talk on the *youth in Asia*, but your topic was *euthanasia*. You may know it better as mercy killing." She said weakly, "I know what euthanasia is," sat down, and after the class was over, immediately dropped it and took another class. Fortunately, embarrassment plus time equals comedy, and by the time Maggie was a senior, she thought that what had happened was funny.

Of course, freshman students don't want other, older students to know that they are new to campus. One of my students carried a campus map in her backpack for her first few days at Ohio University. Whenever she got lost, she would find a building, go into the women's restroom, go into a stall and shut the door, and then look at the map and find out where she was. If any one had seen her consult the map, that person would know that she was a freshman.

Speaking of freshmen, one of my students was from out of state and did not know even a single person in Ohio. She spoke to her sister about being worried that she wouldn't make any friends at Ohio University. Her sister told her, "Don't worry! You'll be fine! Just don't talk to strangers!"

Each summer, lots of incoming students go through freshman orientation at Ohio University. They stay in dorms, go on tours of the campus, and visit the library, among many other things. After the library tour, students get free Freezy-Pops, but librarians tell them that a student first has to ask a question before the members of the tour group get Freezy-Pops. Of course, this encourages students to ask questions about the library; however, once an incoming student, a young woman of wit and intelligence, asked, "Can I have a Freezy-Pop?"

Other students, and their families, are people of wit and intelligence.

When my student Molly Gedeon was still a fetus, her parents had discussions about what to name her, but each parent thought that they had picked a different name. One parent thought she would be named Monica, and the other parent thought she would be named Molly. The name Monica appeared on her birth certificate, but her father insisted on calling her Molly. This created some confusion with friends and teachers because her mother called her Monica and her father called her Molly. On her eighteenth birthday, Monica had her name legally changed to Molly. Her father now calls her Monica.

One of my students was a United States Marine, where he had to take a wilderness survival course that taught him such things as bugs are a very good source of protein if you are trapped without food behind enemy lines. As part of the course, my student and some other soldiers parachuted into the wilderness, where they made good use of their problem-solving skills. As they parachuted into the wilderness, they looked around and noticed a road in the distance. Once they dropped to the earth, they used their compasses to find the road, then they walked into a town and ate pizza.

By the way, when David Bruce, one of the co-authors of this book, was in Navy boot camp, he and the other recruits were sometimes given the order to "Groucho March"! When that happened, he and the other recruits would bend forward, put their hands behind their backs, and in unison do an imitation of comedian Groucho Marx' famous stooped-over walk.

When one of my female students was very young, she had a sister who would sometimes become very naughty and very angry. Once, she was naughty at the dinner table and was sent to bed early while the family continued to eat. My future student heard disturbing noises, thought about a recent nature lesson she had learned at school, and said to her parents, "Mom, Dad, a wolf is in the house." They laughed, and her mother told her, "No, dear, that's just your sister howling with rage."

One of my students was named Rachel. While very young, she attended a day care center that was run by a couple of Jewish women who would say a short Jewish prayer at lunchtime. Rachel learned the prayer, and then she asked her parents at home if she could say a prayer at suppertime. She then recited the Jewish prayer. Her parents were astonished at hearing her speak Hebrew, and she told them, "I figured out our secret. Rachel is a nice Jewish name, and we're Jewish!" (Actually, they were Catholic.)

When they were children, Barbara G. and her sister used to create plays and perform them in front of their parents, who of course were wildly enthusiastic. Unfortunately, after Barbara and her sister grew up, their parents told them how much they dreaded watching those plays.

During a discussion at Ohio University about cheating, OU student Adam C. told a story about a high school student he had known in Indiana. The student had been an exchange student in Japan and knew Japanese well. Adam C. noticed that she had Japanese written on one of her wrists and when he asked her about it, she rolled up her sleeve and showed him that she had Japanese written up to her elbow. Adam C. asked her if she was getting ready to cheat on a test in Japanese, and she replied, "No — biology."

Ohio University student Kimberlee Eichhorn's mother knows sign language. She was once asked to sign the Miranda rights ("You have the right to remain silent ...") at the police station to a person who was deaf and mute. By the way, at a store, Kimberlee once was standing in line behind a little boy and a little girl who plopped 20 pennies and a bunch of candy on the counter. The clerk said, "That'll be $1.20." The little boy looked at the little girl and said, "I don't think we have enough." (Kimberlee gave them the dollar.)

One of my philosophy students saw a slaughtered cow when she was a young child, and as a result she stopped eating meat. Her parents wanted their young daughter to eat animal protein for her health, so they had to convince her to eat meat again. They finally figured out how to do that: they told her that meat grows on trees. (As a young, no-longer-so-naive adult, she became a vegetarian.)

The father of my student Emily Kresiak made a mistake when he proposed to her mother — no, Emily wasn't born yet. He proposed on April Fool's Day. He didn't know it was April Fool's Day, and he was surprised when she laughed at his proposal. Eventually, he learned that it was April Fool's Day, and she learned that he was serious, and Emily is very glad that she said yes.

Nathaniel S. grew up in a household in which the alarm clock was turned up very loud and was set to a radio station. One day, the station was playing a drama show about a fire, and when the alarm went off, the house was filled with the shouts of firemen and the sound of crackling flames. His mother ran screaming through the house, grabbing her children and making sure that they got outside to safety. Only after everyone was outside did they discover what had happened.

Lindsey DeStefano and her sister had separate bedrooms when they were growing up, but they always ended up sleeping in just one of the bedrooms. They used to do such things as scare each other. One sister would go out in the hallway while the other would hide. The sister in the hallway would then enter the room and walk around looking for the other sister, who would jump out from her hiding spot and scare her. They went to bed at an early hour, and part of their bedtime ritual was their father reading them a bedtime story and their mother telling them something each day that they had learned or that they could be proud of. They were scared of monsters, but their father invented "monster spray," which was ordinary water in a spray bottle. He would spray the room and sure enough, no monsters! Once, Lindsey called him back into the room to spray some more because she thought that he had missed a spot.

Rachel Harrison grew up with loving, but mischievous siblings. Her sister was beautiful and popular (so is Rachel), and boys often called her at home. This was before cell phones, and she and the boy would talk on a landline phone that was connected to another phone in the house. Their brother took the other phone, put it on mute, and then went into the bathroom. He then took the phone off mute and flushed the toilet. The boy talking to Rachel's sister asked, "WHERE ARE YOU?"

I would sometimes teach students how to identify sexist and racist and discriminatory language and how to avoid writing it. One of my sample sentences was this: "Irish men are drunks." Of course, I expected a student to identity this as a stereotype, but one of my students struck a blow for feminism by pointing out, "Irish women can be drinks, too."

While in high school, my student Kate K. took a German class. Of course, students would use the word "*herr*" to refer to an adult man, with one exception: Their teacher made them call him "Mister." Why? He did not want them to call him "Herr Ball."

In a class on avoiding clichés and writing vividly, my students would take a cliché and give it a twist to make it a vivid expression. An example I gave my students was Tallulah Bankhead's "I am as pure as the driven slush," which is a variation on "I am as pure as the driven snow." One of my students changed "Better late than never" to "Better late than later."

By the way, I tend to wear what I want. Once I find a comfortable shirt, I will buy several of them and not worry about wearing different styles. However, I used to constantly wear solid-color shirts, but when I found out that my students were making bets on what color of shirt I would wear I did buy a few shirts with stripes of different colors.

One of the goals I had for each of the students in each of my classes was for them to lead lives of wit and intelligence. Many of my students achieved that goal. Of course, Ohio University professors and staff are also witty and intelligent, as seen by the following stories.

When English professor Calvin Thayer talked about Falstaff, the fat rogue living on his wits in Shakespeare's *Henry IV* plays, he would recite a long list of Falstaff's traits: Falstaff is an alcoholic, very fat, a spendthrift, white-bearded, etc. From when I attended Ohio University graduate school, I remember that when Dr. Thayer, who had a white beard, mentioned Falstaff's white beard, he looked shocked, glanced up at his students, and protested, "There's nothing wrong with *that*, of course."

When Baz Luhrmann's *William Shakespeare's Romeo + Juliet* first came out, Shakespeare scholar Samuel Crowl saw it at his local cineplex, where the number of teenyboppers who had come to see Leonardo DiCaprio play Romeo surprised him. When Mr. DiCaprio's Romeo and Claire Danes' Juliet first met, a young DiCaprio fan sitting behind Professor Crowl whispered, "Don't touch him, you bitch."

English professor Frank Fieler knew and loved books. Frequently he would make wise acquisitions for OU's Alden Library. Once, in England, he had almost succeeded in acquiring some important first editions at an auction when a bidder for another university — that was rich because of Texas oil money — spoke up and gave a bid that was twice as large as Dr. Fieler's. The bidder was showing off his university's wealth by waiting until the bidding was almost over, then jumping in with a big bid. Dr. Fieler was so angry that he bid the first editions up until the other fellow's bid was way over the books' true value, then Dr. Fieler stalked out — to the applause of the other people in the auction house.

In the free-wheeling days of the 1960s, Edgar Whan and other English professors used to throw Frisbees in Ellis Hall.

Some students and professors show the haters that they are wrong. Robert DeMott and Dave Smith became friends in the early 1970s. They had a number of things in common that facilitated their friendship: They were or would become editors, scholars, teachers, and writers, plus both had been told as undergraduates by professors that they were "not smart enough or able enough to amount to much in the 'real' world" — predictions that they ignored. Mr. DeMott (actually, Dr. DeMott) became a noted John Steinbeck scholar at Ohio University, and Mr. Smith became a noted poet. By the way, at times, learning excites students. During Spring Quarter of 1970, Dr. DeMott offered a course titled "Writers of the Beat Movement." The course drew so many students that there was standing room only, with many students spilling out of the classroom and into the hallway. Later in 1970, he taught an Honors course on beat poet Gary Snyder — the class met in a teepee on property owned by an OU art professor.

Robert Roe served in the tank corps in Africa during World War II. One day, while driving a tank he ran out of gas in the desert; an Arab saw him and tried to speak to him, but neither spoke the other's language. The Arab shrugged, went to a nearby clump of trees where he had a cache of gasoline, then filled Mr. Roe's tank with gas. Mr. Roe not only reads Old English, but he also reads Marcel Proust in French. As an undergraduate at a time when professors were more autocratic than they are today, he took a French class but had a hard time in it. He needed the professor's permission to drop the class, but when he asked the professor for permission, the professor glowered at him. This so unnerved Mr. Roe that he left the professor's office and learned French.

John Jones specialized in Milton and Swift as an English professor. One day, a freshman student came to Professor Jones' office and asked him why he should take his course. Professor Jones pointed to one bookshelf, then another. "Milton! Swift! What more do you want?"

When English professor Barry Roth first came to OU, he was asked to teach a course on mysteries. But instead of teaching mysteries by such people as Agatha Christie and Rex Stout, he taught such "mysteries" as William Shakespeare's *Hamlet* and William Faulkner's *Sanctuary*.

Classics professor Steve Hays says that he doesn't want his students to graduate only to write poetry to themselves in coffeehouses; humanity can be well served by engineers, journalists, nurses, physicians, dentists, and lawyers. Dr. Hays points out that building a better fuel injector is a wonderful way to serve humanity. When he was taking university classes, he would go through the Student Catalogue and circle the names of professors who had graduated from such schools as Harvard, Yale, and Princeton and then try to take classes from those professors.

OU physiologist Fredrick Hagerman, who worked at NASA, vouches for the authenticity of this anecdote about the first man to walk on the moon: Ohio-born astronaut Neil Armstrong. The first words he spoke on the moon are famous — "One small step for man; one giant leap for mankind" — but he said other things on the moon, including, "Good luck, Mr. Gorsky." At first, people assumed that Mr. Gorsky must be a Russian cosmonaut, but no Russian cosmonaut had that name. For a long time, Mr. Armstrong declined to reveal who Mr. Gorsky was, but after years had passed, he said that the Gorskys had died and so it was OK to reveal the story. It turned out that the Gorskys were next-door neighbors to the Armstrongs when Neil was growing up. One day, during a game, a ball was hit into the Gorskys' yard, and young Neil went to get it. The ball had landed near an open window, and Neil heard the Gorskys arguing. In particular, he heard Mrs. Gorsky yelling, "Sex? You want sex? I'll tell you when you'll get sex! You'll get sex when the kid next door walks on the moon!"

In the 1970s, OU President Claude Sowle decided to hold public meetings at which college deans would argue for money for their departments. Of course, these were spectacular events at which college deans wore caps and gowns and argued passionately for money. At one such public meeting, Dr. Henry Lin, Dean of Fine Arts, began his remarks by saying, "*Ni hao*, Dr. Sowle." Of course, he was speaking flawless Mandarin Chinese, and he continued to speak flawless Mandarin Chinese — which Dr. Sowle did NOT understand — for the rest of his remarks, occasionally using a Chinese abacus to emphasize a financial point. At the end of Dr. Lin's remarks, President Sowle told him, "Henry, you know I don't understand Chinese, but I've never understood you more clearly than right now — you need big bucks!" (By the way, Dr. Lin is the father of Maya Lin, the genius who designed the Vietnam Veterans Memorial in Washington, D.C.)

Artists frequently work with nude models. OU art professor John "Jack" Baldwin and his wife, Bunny, once took a vacation in Mexico, where they went to a clothing-optional beach. Bunny pointed out a particularly beautiful naked woman to Jack, who told her, "Bunny, I am here on vacation. I am not here to work."

An OU art professor once wrote a letter in which she used as many words beginning with the letter F as possible. She called it her F-word letter.

Margaret "Peg" Cohn, Dean Emerita of the Ohio University Honors College, remembers carpooling with other mothers. On one occasion, she had a carload of children when they came across an intersection in which someone had written in large letters a four-letter word beginning with "F" and ending with "K." Ms. Cohn's seven-year-old carefully said each letter aloud, then asked, "Mom?" Ms.

Cohn braced herself, afraid that she would have to give a sex education lesson to a carload of children, but fortunately her seven-year-old asked merely, "How did they do that without getting run over?" Ms. Cohn answered that question, happy that she had remembered "a cardinal rule for parents: Be sure what the question is before you give the answer."

Women's sports and women athletes have not always been respected. For example, in the 1960s (well before Title 9), Catherine L. Brown used to teach field hockey at OU on a field that was also used by ROTC cadets. Sometimes, the ROTC cadets would act as if the women athletes were invisible and march onto the field — even during games. On one occasion when this happened, the ROTC cadets were standing at attention — meaning that they could not move — so Ms. Brown ordered the game to continue, and she rewarded each woman athlete who managed to hit the legs of an ROTC cadet with the ball.

Philosophy professor Warren Ruchti studied under the famous philosopher Nelson Goodman, author of *Ways of Worldmaking* and other important books, at the University of Pennsylvania. Dr. Goodman's intelligence was awesome, and Dr. Ruchti tells several anecdotes about him. A visiting lecturer once was busily writing numerous premises for his arguments on the chalkboard before his lecture when Nelson Goodman walked in. Dr. Goodman glanced at the columns of premises, and then told the visiting lecturer, "You have contradictory premises — look here and here." The lecturer said, "Oh my gosh, you're right!" Another time a visiting lecturer gave a long, involved talk at a colloquium. At the end of the talk, Nelson Goodman looked at Warren Ruchti and said, "He hasn't got the answer," and then walked out of the room. Nelson Goodman moved on to Harvard, from which he retired, but he has not been forgotten. The Ruchtis' family pet was named in honor of the eminent philosopher: Nelson Gooddog.

Many people don't regard reading, writing, and learning as working. Philosophy professor Robert Wieman decided to clean his office one day, so he got sweaty moving furniture around and throwing away heaps of old, outdated files. A maintenance worker passed by and said, "You're the first person I've seen working around here." By the way, Dr. Wieman once told his students, "I have more children than I have fingers, and all but one of them totalled a car by their eighteenth birthday." Also by the way, Dr. Wieman was my main advisor when I was working on my Master's thesis in philosophy. At a volleyball game between philosophy professors and philosophy students, I managed to score a point against him. I noticed that he didn't look too happy about it, so as soon as I could, I let him score a point against me. I could have blocked the ball, but Mama Bruce didn't raise her little boy Davy up to be no fool.

A student once wanted to interview Ohio University zoologist Scott Moody for a term paper on herpes simplex after learning that Dr. Moody taught herpetology. However, herpetologists study amphibians and reptiles, while virologists study viruses such as herpes. Still, the student's mistake was not as bad as it may sound. Interestingly, "herpetology" and "herpes" share a common root word, "herpo," which means crawling. As Dr. Moody explains it, "'Herpeton' means creeping, crawling creature. The earlier naturalists used this term for the slow sprawling terrestrial vertebrates (lizards, snakes, turtles, salamanders) in contrast with the more active terrestrial vertebrates (mammals and birds). The first herpes described scientifically was 'herpes zoster' or shingles. The way a shingles infection manifests itself is as an outbreak of skin rash and blisters that then spread in a linear fashion, hence crawl in one direction. The Greek word 'herpes' was chosen as the genus name for this group of viruses."

Here is a story that Scott Moody tells his friends: "When I was a graduate student living in Germany collecting data for my doctoral dissertation, I often used the public bathroom at the Berlin Train Station. One of the 'sanitary engineers' who happened to be an older woman got her jollies by waiting until there was a long line of men urinating in the contiguous urinal stand, then she would flush real hard, spraying water everywhere, causing men to jump backwards while urinating on the floor or on themselves, displaying their shagadelic [fans of the Austin Powers movies will recognize the reference] tools, and so forth. I witnessed this several times, and it was always the same 'putzfrau.'"

Ohio University sports publicist Frank Morgan occasionally talked at elementary schools about sports. Once he explained that baseballs are made of horsehide, and a horrified little girl exclaimed, "You mean they kill horsies to make baseballs!"

I used to write for *The Athens News* in Athens, Ohio, partly to make extra money and partly to show my composition students that I am a competent writer. I once wrote a preview story for an Ohio University School of Dance performance. The only place for interviews during a rehearsal was in a closet, so Ohio University dance teacher Michele Geller told the dance students, "This is David Bruce. He is going to interview you for a story he is writing for *The Athens News*, so don't be shocked if he asks you to go into a closet with him."

I remember the first article that I wrote for *The Athens News*. It was about the OU women's basketball team and appeared just after Thanksgiving in 1983. I was standing in line at a bank just behind a man who was reading a copy of *The Athens News*. He came to my article, read the headline, and then started to turn the page. I tapped him on the shoulder and said, "Sir, I wrote that article. Please read it."

A janitor at Ohio University is a good problem-solver. OU students aren't supposed to drink soda, coffee, or other liquids in classrooms, but several do anyway — and they leave behind their cans and bottles, creating a huge mess for janitors. One janitor made a statement by collecting all the cans and bottles in each classroom and stacking them up on the professor's desk in the classroom. The next morning the professors reminded their students not to bring liquids to class.

Ohio University engages in problem-solving occasionally. For example, students often create their own paths on a green instead of walking on the concrete sidewalks or brick pathways. Of course, this means that the grass is killed where the students frequently walk. To keep students from creating their own paths, OU groundskeepers sometimes put a load of stinky manure right where the students like to walk.

I mostly enjoyed my years at Ohio University except for the devil students and that time Parking Services booted my car. (What! You couldn't just give me a ticket! OU fundraisers, take note: Don't even think about asking me for money! I gave! This happened years ago, and I still get angry when I think about it.)

The booting of my car happened just after Halloween. Athens, Ohio is reputed to be one of the most haunted places in the world, and when I was a student at Ohio University, some friends and I heard that if you went to a certain place at midnight on Halloween, you would see your future. We followed the directions carefully and arrived at the location exactly at midnight. It was a cemetery.

Now I am retired. The students I wrote about have graduated, and the professors I wrote about have mostly retired or died. I have been spending my retirement happily writing such books as *Dante's* Inferno: *A Retelling in Prose, Virgil's* Aeneid: *A Retelling in Prose*, and *William Shakespeare's* Love's Labor's Lost: *A Retelling in Prose.*

Chapter 2: Down and Out in Athens, Ohio

My Mother

Poverty is not a good thing to experience, but poverty exists and we ought to know about it.

The word "poor" has two meanings: 1) lacking money (impoverished), and 2) lacking quality. I will be writing about poor people, by which I mean people who lack money. I think we all know that some high-quality people don't have a lot of money.

My mother grew up poor in Georgia. She and her brothers and sisters ate a lot of lard sandwiches. A lard sandwich is a slice of bread, spread with lard, and sprinkled with a little sugar, if your family could afford sugar. Often, my mother's parents couldn't afford sugar, and their lard sandwiches were sprinkled with salt.

We would not call this nutritious food, but fat fills the belly, and lard is 100 percent fat — and it was cheap.

Sometimes, my mother and her siblings would steal vegetables from the next-door neighbor's garden. He knew they were stealing vegetables, but he never said anything about it.

For a time, my mother had one dress and one pair of underwear. Once a week, she would stand behind the door, as she called it, take off her dress and underwear and wait until her mother hand-washed them and then let the sun dry them on a clothesline.

Georgia is hot, and in the days before air conditioning — and my mother's family could not have afforded air conditioning even if it had been invented back then — every door and every window was open.

One day when my mother was standing behind the door, her boyfriend came to visit. How old was my mother? Old enough to be embarrassed.

As an adult, one of my mother's first jobs was working in a store that sold clothes, including baby clothes. One day, a woman walked in with a baby. The woman was not well dressed, and the baby was wearing rags. The woman set the baby down on a table displaying baby clothes, stripped the baby, and started putting new clothes on the baby. My mother looked at the woman and knew that she would not be able to pay for the clothing. But my mother helped her dress the baby and then watched as the woman carried the baby out of the store without paying for the new clothing.

One way out of poverty is to marry someone with a job, and my mother got out of poverty by marrying my father.

My Uncle

My mother's brother wanted to escape from poverty, so he tried to run away from it. He stole a car so he could drive up north where he hoped to find opportunity, but he got caught and ended up on a Georgia chain gang for several months. In a chain gang, prisoners are shackled every few feet by the ankles to a long length of chain to keep them from escaping. They work in the hot sun while shackled to the chain, and when they sleep, they are shackled to the bed. No freedom, hard work, hot sun, no pay, bad food, and some mean guards.

When my uncle got released from the chain gang, he hitchhiked up north. He did what a lot of people trying to escape from poverty do: He drifted. He drifted from town to town, seeking opportunity and not finding it. He worked when he could, but the jobs were temporary and low pay. My uncle slept rough often, and he was hungry often. Once, when he was completely broke and completely hungry, he saw a restaurant with a buffet and went inside and asked to speak to the manager. He said, "I am very hungry, I don't have any money, and I would appreciate it very much if you would give me any food that the restaurant is going to throw away. I will be happy to wait by the rear entrance until you are ready to throw away food."

The manager told him to sit down at a table, and then the manager went to the buffet, loaded a big plate high with food, and gave it to him free of charge.

One way out of poverty is to get a good job, and my uncle got out of poverty by getting a job working with sheet metal.

My uncle's work ethic helped him. His employer sent him to California to do some special sheet-metal work, and the people in California wanted to keep him there. They explained that their California employees liked to come to work late, leave early, and take many days off. It was difficult to get someone who would show up and do the work they were supposed to do and were paid to do.

My uncle was also good with money. He got married, bought a house, and raised six children. Each time he made a mortgage payment, he paid extra money so he could pay off the mortgage faster.

If there was a sale on food, he bought lots of it. He had a large pantry, and if there was a sale on peanut butter, two jars for the price of one, he would buy twelve jars and sometimes go back the next day and buy six more jars.

If you went in his pantry — a closet set aside to store food — you saw that it was packed with food. If you went in his kitchen, you saw that he had taken off the doors of the high cabinets in which he stored food so that he could see the food. If you went in his bedroom, you saw that he had all the regular bedroom furniture, but he also had lots of shelves he had installed. The shelves were loaded with things that he had bought on sale that he knew his family could use: food (of course), light bulbs, toothpaste, toilet paper, etc. His bedroom looked like a warehouse.

Once he made a bad purchase: he bought a case of baked beans. Beans are beans, but the sauce they came in can taste good or bad, and the sauce these beans came in tasted bad. His kids told him, "Dad, throw those beans away! They're awful!"

But when you grow up poor, you don't throw beans away. For a long time, whenever my uncle and his family ate baked beans, they ate a mixture of one can of good baked beans and one can of bad baked beans.

My uncle's kids never had to eat lard sandwiches, and neither did I.

My Students and I

I was never the kind of poor that my mother and uncle were, but I did have times when I worked low-wage jobs and could have eaten better. That happens to a lot of people, including college students and people pursuing creative careers. Sometimes, people want be independent and not ask Mom and Dad for help. This can make it hard to both eat good food AND pay the rent.

For a while it seems like I lived on peanut butter-and-jelly cracker sandwiches except that I couldn't afford jelly. I was like my uncle and stocked up on peanut and crackers when they were on sale. I also got bags of apples and bags of carrots occasionally.

Don't think I was hungry. For a while, I worked at a place where I could eat all the doughnuts I wanted, so I weighed 40 pounds more than I do now and resembled the Pillsbury Doughboy.

Once, I was looking forward to getting my paycheck. I like doughnuts and peanut butter and crackers, but eating them every day gets old. I was looking forward to getting my paycheck and eating something good.

I was going to get a sub, and not just any sub — I was going to get a 12-inch sub.

I even wrote a song — songwriters, take note. It goes like this: "I'm going to eat tonight! I'm going to eat tonight!" Repeat 10 or 11 times.

I got my paycheck and it was exactly two cents more than my rent, which was due. So I went to my landlord and signed my paycheck over to him and got two cents back.

My landlord was a nice guy and offered to wait a few more days for the rent, but I turned him down. I didn't have any more money coming in and if I spent my paycheck on food, I wouldn't be able to pay my rent. I did not want to sleep rough.

After paying my rent, I went to my one-room apartment with bath and ate peanut butter and crackers.

Two weeks later, I got another paycheck and ate a 12-inch sub.

I got out of that kind of poverty — which a lot of people go through — by earning my degrees and getting a good job in the OU English Department teaching composition.

Many of my assignments were practical writing because I wanted my students to get jobs when they graduated. My assignments gave students things to talk about at job interviews and papers to add to their writing portfolio.

For example, I assigned a problem-solving letter in which students would write someone and make a recommendation about solving a problem. No one was allowed to write their roommate and recommend that he or she take more showers, but they could write a former manager about ways of increasing profits, raising employee morale, and improving customer satisfaction.

I learned some things from students by reading their assignments, some of which were autobiographical essays. Sometimes I could read between the lines and realize some things that the student may not have realized.

Some of my students wrote about special nights when everyone would eat pancakes for supper. Kids like pancakes with syrup or sprinkled with sugar or spread with peanut butter, so these were really special nights.

If this happens once, then Mom and Dad are probably tired and don't feel like cooking, but sometimes they happened a few nights in a row.

When and where I was growing up, it wasn't unusual for a mother to send a kid over to borrow a cup of flour or a cup of sugar or a couple of eggs. The family was having a special-pancake supper because it was the end of the month and money and food were running low.

Parents really do take special care of their kids. Jerry Clower, a country comedian, remembers that when he was young whenever his mother made chicken, she would tell her kids, "Save the back for me! That's my favorite part!"

Of course, a chicken back is not good eating, and when he got older, he realized that his mother loved her kids and wanted them to eat the best parts of the chicken.

Kids often realize later in life what their parents did for them when the kids were growing up. Sometimes a single mother would sit her kids down at the dinner table, feed them, and not eat. Later, the kids would see her eating peanut butter and crackers. When they got older, they would realize that there wasn't enough good food to go around, so the mother would feed the kids first, eat what they left behind, and then fill up on peanut butter and crackers.

One of my students wrote about one of the best weeks in her life. She was in elementary school, and one day she got off the school bus and went inside her home. The electric lights were off, and her mother and father were wearing jackets inside the house.

Her parents told her that they had a special treat for her: They were going to go camping — in the living room.

They used candles because you don't have electric lights when you go camping, her parents made a tent out of a rope and blankets, and her mother cooked on a tiny portable camp stove that was normally used by backpackers. The "campfire" was twelve tealights (small candles) on plates in the middle of the living room; they cooked marshmallows over those tealights. Her parents sang camp songs and told scary camp stories, and they told family stories about how Mommy and Daddy met and what their little girl was like as a baby. My student had a really fun time camping out in the living room because her parents made it a fun time: She had lots of quantity time and quality time with her parents.

Then one day she came home from school, walked inside her home, and the electric lights were on and the house was warm.

My father made good money as a power lineman, but before he went to lineman school, his job was turning off people's electricity if they couldn't pay their bill. Sometimes, he would knock on the door of a run-down trailer, and a poorly dressed pregnant woman, or a poorly dressed woman holding a baby, or a poorly dressed woman with a couple of toddlers standing behind her would answer the door. Often, the poorly dressed woman wouldn't have the money to pay the electric bill, so my father would tell her that she needed to pay it quickly or her electricity would be cut off. He would then mark on a form that no one was home at the trailer because if no one was home he wasn't allowed to cut off the electricity. He always had to give them a chance to pay their overdue bill, and if they weren't home, they didn't have that chance.

Make no mistake. It's good not to experience poverty, but I think it's good to know what poverty is as long as poverty exists.

Appendix A: About the Author

It was a dark and stormy night. Suddenly a cry rang out, and on a hot summer night in 1954, Josephine, wife of Carl Bruce, gave birth to a boy — me. Unfortunately, this young married couple allowed Reuben Saturday, Josephine's brother, to name their first-born. Reuben, aka "The Joker," decided that Bruce was a nice name, so he decided to name me Bruce Bruce. I have gone by my middle name — David — ever since.

Being named Bruce David Bruce hasn't been all bad. Bank tellers remember me very quickly, so I don't often have to show an ID. It can be fun in charades, also. When I was a counselor as a teenager at Camp Echoing Hills in Warsaw, Ohio, a fellow counselor gave the signs for "sounds like" and "two words," then she pointed to a bruise on her leg twice. Bruise Bruise? Oh yeah, Bruce Bruce is the answer!

Uncle Reuben, by the way, gave me a haircut when I was in kindergarten. He cut my hair short and shaved a small bald spot on the back of my head. My mother wouldn't let me go to school until the bald spot grew out again.

Of all my brothers and sisters (six in all), I am the only transplant to Athens, Ohio. I was born in Newark, Ohio, and have lived all around Southeastern Ohio. However, I moved to Athens to go to Ohio University and have never left.

At Ohio U, I never could make up my mind whether to major in English or Philosophy, so I got a bachelor's degree with a double major in both areas, then I added a Master of Arts degree in English and a Master of Arts degree in Philosophy. Yes, I have my MAMA degree.

Currently, and for a long time to come (I eat fruits and veggies), I am spending my retirement writing books such as *Nadia Comaneci: Perfect 10*, *The Funniest People in Dance*, *Homer's* Iliad: *A Retelling in Prose*, and *William Shakespeare's* Othello: *A Retelling in Prose*.

Appendix B: School Legend: A Short Story

"What are you doing?"

"I think it's pretty clear what I'm doing," my Aunt Clara replied.

She was right.

Clearly, she was using lipstick to color the end of a tampon red.

Aunt Clara said, "Coraline, I think you want to ask *why* I am doing this."

She was right.

I asked, "Why are you using lipstick to color the end of a tampon red?"

"Watch the end of the show tonight, and you'll see why," Aunt Clara answered.

She then taped the red-tipped tampon on her thigh under her skirt.

Aunt Clara is a punk rocker, and she was preparing for a show.

Her all-woman band is called The Blazing Molotovs, and they are locally and regionally known and have no ambition to become nationally and internationally known.

Aunt Clara, aka Clara Molotov, and her bandmates Mara Molotov, Patty Molotov, and Puella Molotov have lives to lead outside music, and as long as they can play most weekends at bars in and around Athens, Ohio, such as the Union, the site of tonight's show, they have no desire to become rich and famous and lead rock star lives.

Aunt Clara once explained, "The dumbest thing I've ever heard is 'Live fast, die young.' I've got stuff to do and a long lifetime is not long enough to do it, much less a short lifetime."

The Blazing Molotovs, as a group, also reject any kind of lifestyle that would slow down their creativity.

"Too many stars — and especially superstars — put out an album every two or three years," Aunt Clara explained to me once. "Not that the Blazing Molotovs ever could be superstars or even stars, but if we were, I hope that we would continue to put out as much music as we want and as we can. I can't imagine writing just one good song every two or three or four months. And I hope that we would never sign a contract that told us what and how much music we could release."

The Blazing Molotovs are very much a Do It Yourself punk band.

They knew each other from Athens High School and like punk fans everywhere, they heard the Ramones, learned to play three chords, and started a band.

Aunt Clara once told me, "The first time we practiced, we wrote a song. We were so excited that we wanted to perform it immediately, so we went to the Union, and the band playing that night let us use their instruments. Halfway through the song, we realized that we had forgotten to write the end of the song, and so the end was a train wreck, but we still got applause from the audience — lots of creative people were in that audience."

In my opinion, although I wasn't there, the Blazing Molotovs performed well that night — just being on stage for the first time is a triumph. Later this night, I got to see the purpose of the red-tipped tampon at the end of a good performance.

The Amazing Molotov Cockgirls finished with an angry song about the patriarchy, toxic masculinity, and misogyny, and then Aunt Clara reached under her skirt, grabbed the red-tipped tampon, held it out so the audience could see it, and yelled, "ARE YOU AFRAID OF WOMEN? YOU SHOULD BE!"

Then she threw the red-tipped tampon into the middle of a group of men.

Fun ensued.

That was Saturday night.

Monday was school at Athens High School, and during lunchtime some of us girls met in one of the girls' bathrooms and discussed a major controversy.

"Did you hear about Susan and Mr. Amorphus?" Beverly asked.

Beverly is someone I would want to be in my band if — when — I start a band.

"No," I said. "What happened?"

"Susan's period started in Mr. Amorphus' English class, and she asked to go to the bathroom. He said no, and she told him that her period had started, and he still wouldn't let her go. He even told her to hold it in and go after class was over. Can you believe it?"

"Hold it in!" I said. "He's an adult. Doesn't he know that periods don't work that way?"

"He's an adult, yes," Beverly said. "But he's a guy, and some guys don't know much about periods — or about women."

"What happened?"

"Susan bled through her pants — just a little and she cleaned it up quickly — and she had to go to the school nurse, who called her mom. Can you imagine the embarrassment?"

Actually, I could. When I was fourteen, I bled through my pants. Fortunately, a kind woman pulled me aside and quietly said to me, "Pardon me, but you have a stain on your pants. Do you need a pad or tampon?"

I already had what I needed, thanks to my mom's insistence on my keeping emergency supplies in my purse *and* in my school backpack. And fortunately, I was wearing a hoodie that I could tie around my waist.

The consensus in the girls' restroom was this: Somebody ought to do something.

I agreed. I was NOT on her period right then, but I wanted to be able to go to the bathroom if I ever had an emergency period situation, just as any girl would.

I also formed a consensus of one: I was the person who ought to do something. Mr. Amorphus was my English teacher, and I had a class with him coming up.

I then affixed some strips of tape to my thigh under my skirt.

The other girls watched me, and they wondered what I was going to do.

I told them, "If you're in English class with me, you'll see. If you aren't in English class with me, you'll hear about it."

In the middle of English class, I raised my hand and asked, "Mr. Amorphus, may I go to the bathroom, please?"

"No, you may not," he said. "Stay here and learn something. Your education is important."

"I agree that my education is important, but my period has started, and I need to go to the bathroom."

"Stay here until the end of class," Mr. Amorphus said. "Just hold it in."

"Periods don't work that way, Mr. Amorphus," I said. "If I stay here, I will bleed through my skirt and onto my seat."

"No, you may NOT go to the bathroom," Mr. Amorphus said.

"OK, Mr. Amorphus," I said.

I took a tampon and a wet wipe out of my purse, and I went to the wastepaper basket in a corner of the classroom.

With Mr. Amorphus and the students, including boys, watching me, I unwrapped the tampon, threw away the wrapper, and spread my legs.

I reached under my skirt and used the strips of tape to securely affix the tampon to my thigh under my skirt.

I threw away the tampon applicator, used the wet wipe to clean my hands, and threw away the used wet wipe.

Then I went to my school desk and sat down.

Mr. Amorphus and some of the boys in class were very red in the face.

Another girl in class raised her hand and asked, "Mr. Amorphus, may I go to the bathroom, please?"

"Of course," Mr. Amorphus said.

Some girls abused the privilege for a while, and then they settled down and behaved correctly.

In that year's school yearbook, I was named "School Legend."

Appendix C: Some Books by Brenda Kennedy (My Sister)

The Forgotten Trilogy
Book One: *Forgetting the Past*
Book Two: *Living for Today*
Book Three: *Seeking the Future*

The Learning to Live Trilogy
Book One: *Learning to Live*
Book Two: *Learning to Trust*
Book Three: *Learning to Love*

The Starting Over Trilogy
Book One: *A New Beginning*
Book Two: *Saving Angel*
Book Three: *Destined to Love*

The Freedom Trilogy
Book One: *Shattered Dreams*
Book Two: *Broken Lives*
Book Three: *Mending Hearts*

The Fighting to Survive Trilogy
Round One: *A Life Worth Fighting*
Round Two: *Against the Odds*
Round Three: *One Last Fight*

The Rose Farm Trilogy
Book One: *Forever Country*
Book Two: *Country Life*
Book Three: *Country Love*

Books in the Seashell Island Stand-alone Series
Book One: *Home on Seashell Island* (Free)
Book Two: *Christmas on Seashell Island*
Book Three: *Living on Seashell Island*

Book Four: *Moving to Seashell Island*

Book Five: *Returning to Seashell Island*

Books in the Pineapple Grove Cozy Murder Mystery Stand-alone Series

Book One: *Murder Behind the Coffeehouse*

Books in the Montgomery Wine Stand-alone Series

Book One: *A Place to Call Home*

Book Two: *In Search of Happiness...* coming soon

Stand-alone books in the "Another Round of Laughter Series" written by Brenda and some of her siblings: Carla Evans, Martha Farmer, Rosa Jones, and David Bruce.

Cupcakes Are Not a Diet Food (Free)

Kids Are Not Always Angels

Aging Is Not for Sissies

Appendix D: Some Books By David Bruce

Retellings of a Classic Work of Literature

Ben Jonson's The Alchemist: *A Retelling*

Ben Jonson's The Arraignment, or Poetaster: *A Retelling*

Ben Jonson's Bartholomew Fair: *A Retelling*

Ben Jonson's The Case is Altered: *A Retelling*

Ben Jonson's Catiline's Conspiracy: *A Retelling*

Ben Jonson's The Devil is an Ass: *A Retelling*

Ben Jonson's Epicene: *A Retelling*

Ben Jonson's Every Man in His Humor: *A Retelling*

Ben Jonson's Every Man Out of His Humor: *A Retelling*

Ben Jonson's The Fountain of Self-Love, or Cynthia's Revels: *A Retelling*

Ben Jonson's The Magnetic Lady, or Humors Reconciled: *A Retelling*

Ben Jonson's The New Inn, or The Light Heart: *A Retelling*

Ben Jonson's Sejanus' Fall: *A Retelling*

Ben Jonson's The Staple of News: *A Retelling*

Ben Jonson's A Tale of a Tub: *A Retelling*

Ben Jonson's Volpone, or the Fox: *A Retelling*

Christopher Marlowe's Complete Plays: Retellings

Christopher Marlowe's Dido, Queen of Carthage: *A Retelling*

Christopher Marlowe's Doctor Faustus: *Retellings of the 1604 A-Text and of the 1616 B-Text*

Christopher Marlowe's Edward II: *A Retelling*

Christopher Marlowe's The Massacre at Paris: *A Retelling*

Christopher Marlowe's The Rich Jew of Malta: *A Retelling*

Christopher Marlowe's Tamburlaine, Parts 1 and 2: *Retellings*

Dante's Divine Comedy: *A Retelling in Prose*

Dante's Inferno: *A Retelling in Prose*

Dante's Purgatory: *A Retelling in Prose*

Dante's Paradise: *A Retelling in Prose*

The Famous Victories of Henry V: *A Retelling*

From the Iliad *to the* Odyssey: *A Retelling in Prose of Quintus of Smyrna's* Posthomerica

George Chapman, Ben Jonson, and John Marston's Eastward Ho! *A Retelling*

George Peele's The Arraignment of Paris: *A Retelling*

George Peele's The Battle of Alcazar: *A Retelling*

George's Peele's David and Bathsheba, and the Tragedy of Absalom: *A Retelling*

George Peele's Edward I: *A Retelling*

George Peele's The Old Wives' Tale: *A Retelling*

George-a-Greene: *A Retelling*

The History of King Leir: *A Retelling*

Homer's Iliad: *A Retelling in Prose*

Homer's Odyssey: *A Retelling in Prose*

J.W. Gent.'s The Valiant Scot: *A Retelling*

Jason and the Argonauts: A Retelling in Prose of Apollonius of Rhodes' Argonautica

John Ford: Eight Plays Translated into Modern English

John Ford's The Broken Heart: *A Retelling*

John Ford's The Fancies, Chaste and Noble: *A Retelling*

John Ford's The Lady's Trial: *A Retelling*

John Ford's The Lover's Melancholy: *A Retelling*

John Ford's Love's Sacrifice: *A Retelling*

John Ford's Perkin Warbeck: *A Retelling*

John Ford's The Queen: *A Retelling*

John Ford's 'Tis Pity She's a Whore: *A Retelling*

John Lyly's Campasne: *A Retelling*

John Lyly's Love's Metamorphosis: *A Retelling*

John Lyly's Sappho and Phao: *A Retelling*

John Webster's The White Devil: *A Retelling*

King Edward III: *A Retelling*

Margaret Cavendish's The Unnatural Tragedy: *A Retelling*

The Merry Devil of Edmonton: *A Retelling*

Robert Greene's Friar Bacon and Friar Bungay: *A Retelling*

The Taming of a Shrew: *A Retelling*

Tarlton's Jests: A Retelling

The Trojan War and Its Aftermath: Four Ancient Epic Poems

Virgil's Aeneid: *A Retelling in Prose*

William Shakespeare's 5 Late Romances: Retellings in Prose

William Shakespeare's 10 Histories: Retellings in Prose

William Shakespeare's 11 Tragedies: Retellings in Prose

William Shakespeare's 12 Comedies: Retellings in Prose

William Shakespeare's 38 Plays: Retellings in Prose

William Shakespeare's 1 Henry IV, aka Henry IV, Part 1: *A Retelling in Prose*

William Shakespeare's 2 Henry IV, aka Henry IV, Part 2: *A Retelling in Prose*

William Shakespeare's 1 Henry VI, aka Henry VI, Part 1: *A Retelling in Prose*

William Shakespeare's 2 Henry VI, aka Henry VI, Part 2: *A Retelling in Prose*

William Shakespeare's 3 Henry VI, aka Henry VI, Part 3: *A Retelling in Prose*

William Shakespeare's All's Well that Ends Well: *A Retelling in Prose*

William Shakespeare's Antony and Cleopatra: *A Retelling in Prose*

William Shakespeare's As You Like It: *A Retelling in Prose*

William Shakespeare's The Comedy of Errors: *A Retelling in Prose*

William Shakespeare's Coriolanus: *A Retelling in Prose*

William Shakespeare's Cymbeline: *A Retelling in Prose*

William Shakespeare's Hamlet: *A Retelling in Prose*

William Shakespeare's Henry V: *A Retelling in Prose*

William Shakespeare's Henry VIII: *A Retelling in Prose*

William Shakespeare's Julius Caesar: *A Retelling in Prose*

William Shakespeare's King John: *A Retelling in Prose*

William Shakespeare's King Lear: *A Retelling in Prose*

William Shakespeare's Love's Labor's Lost: *A Retelling in Prose*

William Shakespeare's Macbeth: *A Retelling in Prose*

William Shakespeare's Measure for Measure: *A Retelling in Prose*

William Shakespeare's The Merchant of Venice: *A Retelling in Prose*

William Shakespeare's The Merry Wives of Windsor: *A Retelling in Prose*

William Shakespeare's A Midsummer Night's Dream: *A Retelling in Prose*

William Shakespeare's Much Ado About Nothing: *A Retelling in Prose*

William Shakespeare's Othello: *A Retelling in Prose*

William Shakespeare's Pericles, Prince of Tyre: *A Retelling in Prose*

William Shakespeare's Richard II: *A Retelling in Prose*

William Shakespeare's Richard III: *A Retelling in Prose*

William Shakespeare's Romeo and Juliet: *A Retelling in Prose*

William Shakespeare's The Taming of the Shrew: *A Retelling in Prose*

William Shakespeare's The Tempest: *A Retelling in Prose*

William Shakespeare's Timon of Athens: *A Retelling in Prose*

William Shakespeare's Titus Andronicus: *A Retelling in Prose*

William Shakespeare's Troilus and Cressida: *A Retelling in Prose*

William Shakespeare's Twelfth Night: *A Retelling in Prose*

William Shakespeare's The Two Gentlemen of Verona: *A Retelling in Prose*

William Shakespeare's The Two Noble Kinsmen: *A Retelling in Prose*

William Shakespeare's The Winter's Tale: *A Retelling in Prose*

Other Fiction

Candide's Two Girlfriends (Adult)

Honey Badger Goes to Hell — and Heaven

I Want to Die — Or Fight Back

The Erotic Adventures of Candide (Adult)

Children's Biography

Nadia Comaneci: Perfect Ten

Personal Finance

How to Manage Your Money: A Guide for the Non-Rich

Anecdote Collections

250 Anecdotes About Opera

250 Anecdotes About Religion

250 Anecdotes About Religion: Volume 2

250 Music Anecdotes

Be a Work of Art: 250 Anecdotes and Stories

The Coolest People in Art: 250 Anecdotes

The Coolest People in the Arts: 250 Anecdotes

The Coolest People in Books: 250 Anecdotes

The Coolest People in Comedy: 250 Anecdotes

Create, Then Take a Break: 250 Anecdotes

Don't Fear the Reaper: 250 Anecdotes

The Funniest People in Art: 250 Anecdotes

The Funniest People in Books: 250 Anecdotes

The Funniest People in Books, Volume 2: 250 Anecdotes

The Funniest People in Books, Volume 3: 250 Anecdotes

The Funniest People in Comedy: 250 Anecdotes

The Funniest People in Dance: 250 Anecdotes

The Funniest People in Families: 250 Anecdotes

The Funniest People in Families, Volume 2: 250 Anecdotes

The Funniest People in Families, Volume 3: 250 Anecdotes

The Funniest People in Families, Volume 4: 250 Anecdotes

The Funniest People in Families, Volume 5: 250 Anecdotes

The Funniest People in Families, Volume 6: 250 Anecdotes

The Funniest People in Movies: 250 Anecdotes

The Funniest People in Music: 250 Anecdotes

The Funniest People in Music, Volume 2: 250 Anecdotes

The Funniest People in Music, Volume 3: 250 Anecdotes

The Funniest People in Neighborhoods: 250 Anecdotes

The Funniest People in Relationships: 250 Anecdotes

The Funniest People in Sports: 250 Anecdotes

The Funniest People in Sports, Volume 2: 250 Anecdotes

The Funniest People in Television and Radio: 250 Anecdotes

The Funniest People in Theater: 250 Anecdotes

The Funniest People Who Live Life: 250 Anecdotes

The Funniest People Who Live Life, Volume 2: 250 Anecdotes

The Kindest People Who Do Good Deeds, Volume 1: 250 Anecdotes

The Kindest People Who Do Good Deeds, Volume 2: 250 Anecdotes

Maximum Cool: 250 Anecdotes

The Most Interesting People in Movies: 250 Anecdotes

The Most Interesting People in Politics and History: 250 Anecdotes

The Most Interesting People in Politics and History, Volume 2: 250 Anecdotes

The Most Interesting People in Politics and History, Volume 3: 250 Anecdotes

The Most Interesting People in Religion: 250 Anecdotes

The Most Interesting People in Sports: 250 Anecdotes

The Most Interesting People Who Live Life: 250 Anecdotes

The Most Interesting People Who Live Life, Volume 2: 250 Anecdotes

Reality is Fabulous: 250 Anecdotes and Stories

Resist Psychic Death: 250 Anecdotes

Seize the Day: 250 Anecdotes and Stories